JESUS ON

MONEY

Book 1 – Charting A New Course

LARRY BURKETT
WITH KAY MOORE

PRODUCTION TEAM

Gene Mims, *President, LifeWay Church Resources*
Michael D. Miller, *Director, Church Leadership Group*
Gary L. Aylor, *Director, Church Stewardship Services*
J. David Carter, *Lead Stewardship Specialist*
Norma J. Goldman, *Editorial Team Leader*
Linda W. Grammer, *Assistant Editor*

ISBN 0-6330-0270-4

Dewey Decimal Classification: 248.6
Subject Heading: JESUS CHRIST—TEACHINGS\STEWARDSHIP\DEVOTIONAL LITERATURE

Printed in the United States of America

Church Stewardship Services
LifeWay Church Resources
127 Ninth Avenue, North
Nashville, TN 37234

TABLE OF CONTENTS

FOREWORD

The Christian of today faces the challenge of living a life that is counter to prevailing culture. Society appears to be terminally ill with the affliction aptly called "affluenza" — the urgent desire to acquire more and more. One symptom is the blending of needs, wants, and desires to the point that there is no discernable difference among the three. Our culture tells us we can have it all, that we deserve it, and we can have it now!

Thoughtful Christians look to the source of truth, God's Word, for guidance in living in this affluent society. What are the guidelines? Is God really concerned with how I manage my resources, and does it have any impact on His plans for me and for the world? What does God expect as I model money management to my family, my church, and the world?

These are tough questions — real questions. And the answers to all of them, plus many more, can be found in the Bible. *Jesus On Money* sets out timeless truths and principles for every area of money management imaginable. The study challenges participants to evaluate behaviors, needs, goals, and purposes in comparison to Bible teachings. Through this study, you will be challenged as never before to bring yourself and your money management practices in line with what God expects of a believer.

If you are already a good manager, this study will help you become an even better one. It will help you model successful money management for your family, extended family, and fellow believers. If you had no role model, or never learned practical how-tos in dealing with finances, *Jesus On Money* is for you. If you are hopelessly in debt, this study will show you how to get out and stay out.

We are praying that your life, your church, and the Kingdom will be blessed as you seek God's plan in managing all He has entrusted to your care. The prize — "Well done, good and faithful servant" — is well worth the cost!

Gary L. Aylor, Director
Church Stewardship Services

JESUS ON

MONEY

Charting A New Course

INTRODUCTION

Scripture Verses

"This day I call heaven and earth as witnesses against you that I have set before you life and death, blessings and curses. Now choose life, so that you and your children may live."
— Deuteronomy 30:19

"When Jesus heard this, he said to him, 'You still lack one thing. Sell everything you have and give to the poor, and you will have treasure in heaven. Then come, follow me.'"
— Luke 18:22

"But if serving the Lord seems undesirable to you, then choose for yourselves this day whom you will serve, whether the gods your forefathers served beyond the River, or the gods of the Amorites, in whose land you are living. But as for me and my household, we will serve the Lord."
— Joshua 24:15

"Therefore, since we are surrounded by such a great cloud of witnesses, let us throw off everything that hinders and the sin that so easily entangles, and let us run with perseverance the race marked out for us."
— Hebrews 12:1

F requently the Bible records God calling His people to make decisions. Moses challenged Israel to choose between life and death (Deuteronomy 30:19). Jesus challenged the rich young ruler to sell all that he had, give to the poor, and follow Him (Luke 18:22). Joshua 24:15 carries the idea of coming to a deciding point. (See the verses at left.)

Although you can never earn God's love, making decisions that are consistent with His Word will result in greater blessing, joy, and peace. God's finest blessings are reserved for those who apply His Word to *all* areas of life, including money management.

Unfortunately, many people have become entangled in lifestyles that result in financial bondage. Hebrews 12:1 speaks to these entanglements. Entangled people are no longer totally free to serve Him. For instance, did you know that:

- Money is the leading cause of conflict in marriage?[1]
- Americans presently spend $1.20 for every $1.00 earned?[2]
- One in three born-again Christians say they find getting ahead in life to be impossible because of the financial debt they have incurred?[3]
- Americans now save at the lowest rate since the Great Depression: 0.5 percent, or $5.00 for every $1,000 earned?[4]

I want to congratulate you for making the decision to join the small-group study called *Jesus On Money: Charting a New Course*. During the next six weeks, you will discover solutions to the following three fundamental issues:

- How to know if you're taking on too much debt
- How to get out of debt
- How to stay out of debt

By faithfully completing the exercises in this workbook, you will take the first, critical step toward experiencing *financial freedom*. You can make financial decisions that are consistent with God's plan for your life. These decisions will result in peace and joy. You may not be in debt but are taking this course to prevent future problems. Congratulations again! You will gain much insight that will help you know what to do if you start to stray from a Christlike path of money management.

Plan now to study all three books in this series. Book 2, called *Jesus On Money: Making Mid-Course Corrections*, covers topics such as financial planning, investing, saving, contentment, business relationships, and making career changes. Make corrections in these areas based on God's truth, and you will become established in the lifestyle of a faithful steward for God. Book 3, called *Jesus On Money: Crossing the Finish Line*, explores how to deal with abundance, leave a godly legacy, and use your resources to partner with God in Great Commission work.

You may be facing some discouraging financial circumstances, but where God is, hope always exists. The apostle Paul once declared, "Now to Him who is able to do immeasurably more than all we ask or imagine, according to his power that is at work within us, to him be glory in the church and in Christ Jesus throughout all generations, for ever and ever! Amen" (Ephesians 3:20-21). Because that is true, you can expect great things from God as you enter this study. In faith, ask Him to lead you into profound changes in the way you view money and material things so that His name will be glorified through you!

The *Jesus On Money* study employs an interactive learning process. Each day, for five days a week, you are asked to study a segment of the material and complete activities that relate to what you just read. Each day's work requires 20 to 30 minutes of study time. Even if you find that you can study the material in less time, spread out the study over five days. This will give you more time to apply the truths to your life.

At the end of each week's study, members gather for group sessions. The sessions help you reflect on the concepts and experiences presented in *Jesus On Money* and apply them to your life. You will share insights gained, look for answers to problems encountered, and gain strength from the fact that others encounter similar struggles and victories.

Although you may benefit from completing the studies totally on your own, without a group experience you will have missed the critical element Jesus' disciples experienced: relationships with one another in Christ's presence. As members share their own testimonies about growing in stewardship, others give feedback and are encouraged in their own challenges and victories. Therefore, I strongly encourage you to connect with other believers to study this material.

INTRODUCTION *continued . . .*

Notes

This book has been written as a tutorial text. Study it as if I were sitting at your side, helping you learn. When I ask you a question or give you an assignment, respond immediately. Each assignment appears in **boldface type**. As your personal tutor, I will give you some feedback about your response — for example, a suggestion about what you might have written. This process is designed to help you learn the material more effectively. Do not deny yourself valuable learning by skipping the learning activities.

Set a definite time and select a quiet place where you can study with little interruption. Keep a Bible handy for times when the material asks you to look up Scripture. Make notes of problems, questions, or concerns that arise as you study. You will discuss many of these during your group sessions. Write your notes in the margins of this book so you can find them easily.

If you have started a study of *Jesus On Money* and you are not involved in a group study, try to enlist some friends or associates who will work through this course with you. A husband and wife are encouraged to work through the material together. *Jesus On Money Leader Guide* provides guidance and learning activities for these sessions. (Send orders or inquiries to Customer Service Center, 127 Ninth Avenue, North; Nashville, TN 37234; call 1-800-458-2772, or visit your local LifeWay Christian Store. Ask for ISBN 0-6330-0308-5.)

Key to this study is the decision to trust Jesus as your Savior. If you have not done this already, I encourage you to make this decision as the study begins. Within the Week 1 work you will find helps in making that decision. You will benefit more from this course if you go through the material already having committed your life to Christ. If you're not ready to make that decision just now, be aware that the need for this decision will be an ongoing emphasis. The material gives you opportunity to look at your relationship with Christ and to determine your need to commit your life to Him.

Before your first group session, you will be asked to complete two practical assignments: (1) identifying every outstanding debt you have, and then (2) accounting for 100 percent of your take-home income. (See the charts on pages 120-122.) Ideally, you would complete these steps before the first group session begins. However, I recognize that it may take several weeks before you can fully get tabs on where every cent of your money goes each month. If you aren't able to complete this task by group session 1, continue to add the missing pieces until you have the total picture. By the time of your Week 4 work, when you are asked to draft a working budget, you will need to have a clear picture of where your money is spent.

A final word: this study is not designed for those who want a quick fix but for those who are willing to undergo a life change. In the absence of a clear commitment to living by God's principles, people typically revert to old spending patterns once the "heat" is off and pressures let up. Ask yourself, "Is my goal to live for God and honor Him with all areas of my life, including my finances, or just to relieve the financial pressure by getting out of debt?"

Please know that I am much in prayer for the members of the body of Christ who are studying this material. I pray that God will use it to help you live the abundant life that Jesus describes in John 10:10, at right.

Larry Burkett

[1] www.nccs.org
[2] Gerri Detweiler, "How to Manage Your Money" radio program, Christian Financial Concepts, 3/24/99.
[3] www.barna.org
[4] Robert Samuelson, "Hell No, We Won't Save," *The Washington Post*, 2/17/99, p. A17.

Scripture Verses

"The thief comes only to steal and kill and destroy; I have come that they may have life, and have it to the full."
— John 10:10

JESUS SAID...

Week 1, Day 1

WHAT "HEALTHY" LOOKS LIKE

Scripture Verses

"The earth is the Lord's, and everything in it, the world, and all who live in it."
        —*Psalm 24:1*

"You made him ruler over the works of your hands; you put everything under his feet."
        —*Psalm 8:6*

"No one can serve two masters. Either he will hate the one and love the other, or he will be devoted to the one and despise the other. You cannot serve both God and Money."
        —*Matthew 6:24*

You've probably heard about the man who didn't realize how badly his head hurt until he stopped banging it against the wall. Many people — yes, even those who serve God faithfully as His followers — are like that man. Some harmful patterns in their lives have gone on for so long and are so much a part of their behavior that they have forgotten, or possibly never knew, what "healthy" looks like. Improper use of God's resources is so ingrained they may not even realize that they are headed down the wrong path and have been for years.

Fortunately, you have a much better way to identify what kind of course you are charting than this individual did. God provides His Word as a plumb line to determine where you stand in relationship to the way He wants you to live. That's why I call this study *Jesus On Money*. Jesus is the Word and the source of solutions for all of life's problems — including monetary ones. More than seven hundred Scripture references directly relate to our use of money.

What are God's basics to help you diagnose your own situation? For starters, Psalm 24:1, appearing in the margin, describes how God views His relationship to your possessions — He is the true owner of everything. You possess only what He entrusts to you. You are like a secondary owner. You may use and enjoy responsibly what God entrusts to you, but the bottom line is: everything is His anyway. He owns the entire 100 percent — not just the tenth that people return to Him in the offering plate on Sundays. A Christian must acknowledge this truth, consciously transferring ownership of every possession to God. That means money, time, family, material possessions, education, and even earning potential for the future. This acknowledgement of ownership is essential to experience the Spirit-filled life in the area of finances. See Psalm 8:6.

Does this make sense to you? Do you actually ever think about that paycheck you receive, that grocery money you must stretch until next payday, the interest you receive on your savings account, the dwelling that provides your shelter, even the tube of toothpaste in your cabinet, as being directly issued to you by God? Do you realize that you're answerable to Him for decisions you make about these items — and everything else you own, as well?

Week 1, Day 1

Check the statement below that best describes how you reacted when you read the two previous paragraphs.

❑ 1. This seems a little far-fetched to me. I've worked hard for what I own. I don't need to answer to anyone for how I use my possessions.

❑ 2. Why should God care about what I do with my money? He's so far away and remote. Trivia, like where my dollars go, can't possibly matter to Him. He has more important things to worry about, like wars and famines and hurricanes.

❑ 3. I know what you're talking about, this personal responsibility issue with my possessions. But I have too many financial obligations at the moment to think about how God should be involved.

❑ 4. I'd like to have better financial accountability, but my patterns have been part of me for too long. I'm a hopeless "spendaholic" and can't change.

❑ 5. The concept of God's owning everything is highly important to me. With each purchase or investment, I try to ask myself whether God would be pleased with the decision I just made.

If you checked any of these statements except the last one, chances are you need to adjust your outlook and habits. Failing to be constantly aware that God is the owner and you are merely the steward may well indicate some attitudes and patterns that have created debt. The concept that our things belong to us and not to God is one of the most devious schemes Satan ever invented.

If you checked the last box, great! You're likely on the right track as you run the race. But this course can still help you as you look for strategies to stay out of debt and to affirm what you're already doing as a good steward. As Proverbs 22:3 says, "A prudent man sees danger and takes refuge, but the simple keep going and suffer for it." Don't take this study lightly!

JESUS SAID...

WHAT "HEALTHY" LOOKS LIKE *continued*...

Scripture Verses

Carry this exercise one step further. If someone had an attitude that caused him or her to check one of the first four answers, how could this create a climate for overspending that leads to debt?

Focus in on one of the first four statements (even if you didn't check one of them.) Tell below how the attitude described in that statement could lead someone to a lifestyle encumbered by debt.

_____

_____

_____

_____

_____

For example, if you chose to comment on statement #1 (I've worked hard for what I own and don't need to take anyone else into consideration), you might have replied something like this: Failing to think about God when I make a purchase can lead me to respond to my own need for instant gratification rather than prompting me to ask how this purchase fits into God's big picture for me. You might continue to acquire things on this basis until your financial obligations are tremendous.

Read John 10:10b in the margin. At the end of the introductory material, I mentioned "the abundant life" Jesus promised. Describe below what having this type of life means to you.

"I have come that they may have life, and have it to the full."
—*John 10:10b*

_____

_____

_____

_____

_____

Week 1, Day 1

Notes

Clearly the Bible indicates that God wants you to live abundantly, but Satan wants just the opposite for you. Make no mistake. Satan desires to diminish and, if possible, destroy your Christian witness through financial bondage. Taking these concepts seriously and allowing God to speak to your heart will put you on the path to live "the abundant life" — without the bondage of debt-producing habits.

Stop and pray; ask God to keep you conscious of His ownership of all things as you make each financial decision.

JESUS SAID...

HOW DID I GET THIS WAY?

In trying to get some idea of what normal is — or making sure you stay on track if you believe you already have sound financial practices in place — it helps to continually ask yourself the question, "How did I get this way?" Insight into the attitudes and habits that have created your current condition is the best way to start getting yourself untangled and set onto a new path.

In the introductory session, you were asked to begin working on two practical assignments: identifying every outstanding debt you have and then accounting for 100 percent of your take-home income. If you haven't finished these assignments yet, continue to add the missing pieces. In that process, perhaps you've already turned up some nuts-and-bolts answers about how your current circumstance developed. Although you'll look in more detail in Week 3 about areas where overspending may occur, you may already be able to testify, "Oops. I now know that I'm spending more than I really can afford to pay monthly for my house." Or, "I can see I should have stopped last month before I overspent on all those clothing purchases."

Write down an early assessment of yourself financially. If you've uncovered some practices you're not pleased with, ask yourself the question, "How did I get this way?" Briefly describe below.

_____

_____

_____

_____

_____

_____

In future weeks, you'll be asked more specific questions about your financial assessment, and you'll learn some practical tips. But for now, let's continue to look at what may be spiritually behind an out-of-control pattern of overspending.

Week 1, Day 2

In Day 1 we looked at four harmful statements that represent the way many people look at God's involvement with their finances. In a nutshell, again, the four were:

1. I've worked hard for my money and my possessions. I don't need to answer to anyone for how I use them.
2. God's too far away and remote to care where my dollars go.
3. I'm too overwhelmed at the moment to care how God is involved in my finances.
4. My patterns have been a part of me for too long. I'm hopeless and can't change.

Let's now turn to the second of these — the concept that God is too far away and remote to care about your personal spending. What does God's Word say?

Look at the last three verses in the margin. Read the verses, then summarize below what the verses reveal about God's availability to you. If you can recall some other Scriptures that assure you of God's nearness and concern, jot down their references here also.

_____

_____

_____

_____

_____

_____

Sometimes people think God couldn't possibly care about them because their earthly parents — their first role-models — were distant, far away, and disinterested. It's easy to stereotype God in a negative role because of how your mother and/or father — your first representations of God as parent — may have related to you.

Scripture Verses

"No one can serve two masters. Either he will hate the one and love the other, or he will be devoted to the one and despise the other. You cannot serve both God and Money."
—Matthew 6:24

"So they pulled their boats up on shore, left everything and followed him."
—Luke 5:11

"God is our refuge and strength, an ever-present help in trouble."
—Psalm 46:1

"The Lord will watch over your coming and going both now and forevermore."
—Psalm 121:8

"You are near, O Lord, and all your commands are true."
—Psalm 119:151

JESUS SAID...

HOW DID I GET THIS WAY? *continued . . .*

Notes

Does this previous statement apply to you and your family? ❑ **Yes** ❑ **No**
If you answered yes, describe the situation.

_____

_____

_____

_____

_____

_____

Although your heart-knowledge of God might tell you otherwise, God is Who the Bible says He is. He is actively involved in your life, even down to your dollars and cents and balance sheets. Everything that goes on in your life matters to Him, and He's as close to you as a prayer.

Below, write a prayer that summarizes your desire to feel that God knows and cares. You might write something like this: "Dear God, I know Your Word says You are intimately involved with me. Help me to cling to this truth and to use this knowledge to guide my financial decisions." After you write it, pray it aloud.

_____

_____

_____

_____

_____

_____

_____

_____

Week 1, Day 2

Notes

What is Jesus saying to you today about where you are with respect to money?

_____

_____

_____

_____

_____

Review the Scriptures referenced in Day 1 and Day 2. Write down the verse that really speaks to where you are right now.

_____

_____

_____

_____

_____

JESUS SAID...

This Week

Scripture Verses

"My tears have been my food day and night, while men say to me all day long, 'Where is your God?' These things I remember as I pour out my soul."
　　　　　—Psalm 42:3-4

"He lifted me out of the slimy pit, out of the mud and mire; he set my feet on a rock and gave me a firm place to stand."
　　　　　—Psalm 40:2

"Though I walk in the midst of trouble, you preserve my life."
　　　　　—Psalm 138:7

GOD'S ROLE IN THE PROCESS

Let's continue with the other two statements you first saw in Day 1. Does statement 3 or statement 4 apply to you?

3.   I'm too overwhelmed at the moment to care about how God is involved in my finances.
4.   My patterns have been a part of me for too long. I'm hopeless and can't change.

Too overwhelmed! Most of us can certainly relate to that feeling, at one time or the other. Bills pile in, and we hardly have time to sit down and pay them, much less to consider whether this monthly pile of bad news matters to God. But being overwhelmed — and failing to consider God's role — may be the very thing that perpetuates the cycle.

What does the Bible say about God's awareness of that perpetually overwhelmed feeling? Read the verses in the margin. Underline any statements in them with which you can identify.

This "snowed-under" feeling you have was acknowledged in God's Word centuries ago. God wants you to be aware of Him in these overwhelming times so you can pour out your soul to Him, as the psalmist did, and rely on Him for preservation.

Hopeless, helpless. It's easy to look at past financial failures and believe that things just can't get better. You can get caught up in the blame game — blaming yourself or others for bad planning or wrong decisions. Past failures can govern how you view yourself — as worthless and incapable. Shame can impact you tremendously if you believe you can never be different from what you have been.

The story of Zacchaeus illustrates the biblical premise of regeneration — the new birth that you experienced in Christ when you trusted Him as Savior (and an entirely new person in terms of money beliefs!). Read this Bible story in Luke 19: 1-10. What caused the dramatic change? Describe in the space on the next page.

Week 1, Day 3

_____

_____

_____

_____

_____

Scripture Verses

In Christ you are unconditionally loved and accepted. God sent His Son to die for you so all your past wrongdoings are wiped from God's memory when you seek forgiveness. You experience a rebirth, just as Zacchaeus did. Allowing a debt cycle to continue just because you feel bound by a past history of overspending doesn't take into account God's ability to regenerate and transform.

Below, describe what you would be like as a modern-day, renewed Zacchaeus in terms of your finances. What would it feel like to see yourself as a new creation — free of the patterns that have shackled you?

"It will be good for that servant whose master finds him doing so when he returns. I tell you the truth, he will put him in charge of all his possessions."
—*Matt. 24:46-47*

_____

_____

_____

_____

_____

Stop and pray, asking God to help you make the above description possible.

As you read and interact with this material, you may also be thinking to yourself, "I'm not sure I've had that rebirth — that experience of regeneration and renewal that the study just mentioned." Before you go any further in

". . . for all have sinned and fall short of the glory of God . . . ."
—*Romans 3:23*

JESUS SAID...

GOD'S ROLE IN THE PROCESS *continued . . .*

Scripture Verses

"For by grace you have been saved through faith, and that not of yourselves; it is the gift of God, not of works, lest anyone should boast."
　　　　—Ephesians 2:8-9

"But God demonstrates His own love toward us, in that while we were still sinners, Christ died for us."
　　　　—Romans 5:8

"Therefore, since we have been justified through faith, we have peace with God through our Lord Jesus Christ . . . . And hope does not disappoint us, because God has poured out his love into our hearts by the Holy Spirit, whom he has given us."
　　　　—Romans 5:1, 5

Jesus On Money, it's highly important to get that matter settled, or what you learn here will be worthless to you. Stop for a moment and decide in your own heart and mind about your relationship with Jesus Christ. Ask yourself the question, *Have I accepted Jesus as my Lord and my Savior?* Without the free gift of salvation that is found only in Jesus Christ, you do not possess the Holy Spirit. Without the Holy Spirit, you can't gain understanding into what God's Word says about finances or any other subject.

Salvation is the free gift from God that comes to you when you accept in your heart and mind that Jesus Christ died for you as a sinner, when you confess that He is the Lord of your life, and when you believe that He is alive and has conquered sin and death for you.

Call on the Lord, using the following prayer or one in your own words: *Dear God, I know that Jesus is Your Son and that He died on the cross and was raised from the dead. I know that I am a sinner and need forgiveness. I am willing to turn from my sins and trust Jesus as my Savior and Lord. Thank You for saving me. In Jesus' name. Amen.*

If you prayed that prayer just now, welcome to the family of God! You have made the most important decision of your life. You can be sure you are saved and have eternal life. Talk to your pastor, a Christian friend, or your *Jesus On Money* group leader about your decision. If you are already a Christian, pause and thank God for new life in Christ. Ask Him to help you exhibit the qualities of "a new creation."

Week I, Day 3

Notes

JESUS SAID...

This Week

Day 1:   What "Healthy" Looks Like
Day 2:   How Did I Get This Way?
Day 3:   God's Role in the Process
Day 4:   How "Things" Demand Attention
Day 5:   Putting Feet to Your Faith

Scripture Verses

"For he chose us in him before the creation of the world . . . ."
　　　　—Ephesians 1:4a

"For you created my inmost being; you knit me together in my mother's womb. I praise you because I am fearfully and wonderfully made; your works are wonderful, I know that full well. My frame was not hidden from you when I was made in the secret place. When I was woven together in the depths of the earth, your eyes saw my unformed body. All the days ordained for me were written in your book before one of them came to be."　*—Psalm 139:13-16*

"For God so loved the world that he gave his one and only Son, that whoever believes in him shall not perish but have eternal life."　　*—John 3:16*

HOW "THINGS" DEMAND ATTENTION

You can continue answering the question, "How did I get this way?" by looking at the role things have in your life and discovering how things demand attention. An exalted value of "things" is a sure-fire warning flag that you may be in financial trouble. Have "things," or your possessions, ever been the rudder that steered your ship?

Fill in the blanks with words or phrases that may indicate how you have felt in the past about possessions.

If I could only own _____, my life would be much better. I'm unhappy with myself because I don't have a _____. People would think of me more highly if I just possessed _____.

A man once lamented that he'd be much better off financially if it weren't for the extravagance of his neighbors! You may allow someone else's material goods to determine just how important possessions are to you.

Incidentally, although your focus in this study centers largely on money and how you use it, you could also substitute persons or purposes in an exercise like the one above. Many times, people think that looking a certain way, achieving a certain goal, or gaining the approval of certain persons is their "be-all, end-all." They think these matters sum up their identity.

God's Word addresses this, too. Read the verses appearing in the margin. Then answer the questions.

What do the verses say about how important you are to God?

_____

_____

_____

In Christ we are all financially equal. The things of this world will quickly pass away, and death will remove all wealth from us. God will never use money in our lives to build our egos. Skim through the book of James and see the clear admonition not to fawn over the wealthy.

Week 1, Day 4

If you could constantly remember how worthy you are in God's eyes, how do you think that would impact your spending habits?

_____

_____

_____

_____

How could an exalted view of "things" lead a person into harmful debt?

_____

_____

_____

_____

You may have come to equate importance with living in a large home on the fashionable side of town or wearing name-brand clothing. The danger of defining yourself by temporal things is that they eventually fade away. Take away the nice things, and who are you?

The verses you read reveal some lasting truths about who you are as God's child. God involved Himself in your creation. He has waited patiently for your arrival on the scene because you have unique contributions to make to life. Most importantly, He sent His Son to die for you. He went to a whole lot of trouble for you.

What you achieve or own doesn't determine what you are. Even without the temporal things you listed, you have a unique identity in Christ. You are a person of worth because He says so.

Identify a friend, family member, or your regular prayer partner who will pray with you about this. Ask that person to pray that you will always look to Christ for your worth instead of to things.

Scripture Verses

"And do not seek what you should eat or what you should drink, nor have an anxious mind. For all these things the nations of the world seek after, and your Father knows that you need these things. But seek the kingdom of God, and all these things shall be added to you. For where your treasure is, there your heart will be also."
—Luke 12: 29-31, 34

JESUS SAID...

Week 1, Day 5

Scripture Verses

"Let them do good, that they be rich in good works, ready to give, willing to share, storing up for themselves a good foundation for the time to come, that they may lay hold on eternal life."
—1 Timothy 6:18-19

PUTTING FEET TO YOUR FAITH

Conclude this week's work by putting some of these concepts into practice. If you truly operated from some of the healthy premises you've studied, how would that guide your attitude toward money?

Read the following case studies. Describe the decision the person might make about money if he or she remembered —

   (1) God ultimately owns everything and cares about the choices you make about finances;

   (2) Your identity is in Christ and not in possessions or achievements.

Fellow singles coaxed Jenny to go with them on a cruise. Jenny felt torn between joining them and paying off some college tuition loans that she had set as a goal to wipe out within a year. She also had felt led to sign up for a church mission trip that was organizing for a year from now.

_____

_____

_____

_____

Amy loved clothes and had an ample wardrobe. If Amy had a bad day, nothing cheered her as much as heading for the shopping mall after work. Credit-card bills mounted as a result of Amy's habit. She eased her guilt by contending she deserved her new clothes because of the cantankerous boss she had to endure.

_____

_____

_____

_____

Week 1, Day 5

Fred collected World War II memorabilia — a fun hobby that soon grew to an obsession. Pictures, books, and artifacts filled every corner of his home. Every weekend Fred spent time away from his family as he attended collectors' shows and exhibits.

_____

_____

_____

_____

Susan's goal was to learn to live within her income and stop spending more than she made. Her office was sponsoring a covered-dish luncheon. Susan thought it would be impressive to take a taco salad, but she had already spent the money allotted for groceries for the week. She tried to rationalize using her credit card for the ingredients by saying the luncheon was a really special occasion for her boss' birthday.

_____

_____

_____

_____

You might have chosen responses similar to these: Saying "No" to peer pressure is tough, but if Jenny's goal truly is to be debt-free, she would delay her gratification and say "No" to the cruise plans until she reaches her goal. Then she could decide how to fund the mission trip that God was leading her to do. Amy was using things to meet an inner emptiness and to cover it over with clothing purchases. Remembering that God's approval of her is most important could help her overcome her spending habit, even when she feels the censure of others. Fred would benefit from study of the concepts in the *How Much Is Enough? Devotional Guide*,[1] in which participants learn Christ-honoring limits to their drive to acquire and spend. Determining what dish

JESUS SAID...

Notes

PUTTING FEET TO YOUR FAITH *continued . . .*

she could prepare with ingredients on hand could keep Susan from over-spending and cause her to be a good steward of the food already in the pantry.

Have you ever found yourself in situations like that of Jenny, Amy, Fred, and Susan? If so, you might catch a glimpse of how debt has crept up on you.

The good news is, none of these habits is impossible to correct! Philippians 4:13 says "I can do everything through him who gives me strength." God knows, God cares, and God's love for you is paramount. Hopefully these three statements, which sum up this week's work, will undergird you as you continue to chart a new course and will help you listen to what Jesus would say to you about money.

Ask God to remind you that your ability to be disciplined about money is included in the "can-do" promise of Philippians 4:13. Ask Him to pour strength into you in future days as you seek to set aside harmful habits.

Write down two things that you believe Jesus has said to you this week about money.

_____

_____

_____

_____

_____

[1] To order *How Much Is Enough? Devotional Guide* or other related products, write to Customer Service Center, 127 Ninth Avenue, North; Nashville, TN 37234; call 1-800-458-2772; or visit your local LifeWay Christian store.

How Much Is Enough? 30 Days to Personal Revival 0-7673-9559-X (Devotional Guide)

Continued on next page . . .

Week 1, Day 5

How Much Is Enough? Video   0-7673-9563-8
How Much Is Enough? Training Kit   0-7673-9560-3
How Much Is Enough? Poster   0-7673-9562-X
How Much Is Enough? Bulletin Insert 0-7673-9561-1

Notes

JESUS SAID...

PATTERNS RUN DEEP

Scripture Verses

"I spoke to you in your prosperity, But you said, 'I will not hear.' This has been your manner from your youth, That you did not obey My voice."
—Jeremiah 22:21

"Therefore I will give their wives to others, And their fields to those who will inherit them; Because from the least even to the greatest Everyone is given to covetousness; From the prophet even to the priest Everyone deals falsely."
—Jeremiah 8:10

"Now it shall be, if you will diligently obey the Lord your God, being careful to do all His commandments which I command you today, the Lord your God will set you high above all the nations of the earth."
—Deuteronomy 28:1

Most people who find themselves mired in debt will pinpoint an economic slump within their businesses, communities, regions, or nation, as the start of their financial problems. But, as you studied in Week 1, these woes usually appear long before an economic downturn. The root causes may have begun years earlier — perhaps even in childhood.

The truth is, families don't experience more problems during economic slumps or struggles. They suffer more *symptoms*. The symptom may be unpaid bills, and the consequence may be that their utilities are turned off or their cars are repossessed. But many of the symptoms that occur so frequently today — business failures, massive bankruptcies, divorce, and families who hold three or four jobs to make ends meet — stem back to the same basic problem of ignoring God's Word and His warnings.

Do you attribute your current financial circumstance to an event, such as those mentioned above? If so, describe the event below.

_____

_____

_____

_____

Read the last verse in the margin. God's instructions are neither complicated nor harsh. In fact, they are designed to free you, not bind you to a set of rigid do's and don'ts. The difficulty is that most American families have been duped into a life of "get-rich-quick" outlooks that include the way they buy homes, cars, clothes, and food. For the last forty years, God's principles in the area of finances have been largely ignored. People are now reaping what they have sown.

An article in a business magazine vividly brought this into focus. The largest mail-order seed company in the country decided to go out of business, despite the fact that sales were higher than ever. Unfortunately, so were nonpayments by its mail-order sales force. For nearly fifty years, the company had supplied seeds to children who sold them door-to-door, mostly in rural communities, to raise money. In recent years, the nonpayment rate to the company had risen

Week 2, Day 1

Scripture Verses

"Therefore if you have not been faithful in the unrighteous mammon, who will commit to your trust the true riches? And if you have not been faithful in what is another man's, who will give you what is your own?"

—Luke 16:11-12

"A righteous man who walks in his integrity — How blessed are his sons after him."

—Proverbs 20:7

steadily, until in 1981 it reached 70 percent. The average age of these delinquent salespeople was 10 years! The final straw occurred when the company attempted to contact the parents, hoping the parents would help in the collection, only to discover that the parents actually encouraged the children to keep the money.

The symptom described is nonpayment of a just debt, but the problem runs much deeper. It involves basic values that parents fail to instill in their children. It manifests itself in an attitude that asserts "my rights come before others'." Parents' lack of integrity is reflected and amplified in their children's lives. Unfortunately, later these parents probably won't understand why irresponsible children become irresponsible adults. The verse from Proverbs appearing in the margin reminds you of your responsibility to future generations.

As you read the above paragraphs about parental modeling, do some scenes from your childhood come to mind? Below please sum up your parents' attitudes about money. For example, if you grew up in a family in which payment of debt was ignored or trivialized as has been illustrated here, please describe.

_____

_____

_____

_____

_____

Frequently in this study, I may ask you to reflect on ways that your attitudes about money or self are ingrained through your upbringing. When this happens, the purpose is not to encourage you to blame or to hold hostile, bitter attitudes about the home in which you were reared. These questions are to help you gain insight, so destructive patterns don't continue into a future generation.

If you've already repeated some of these patterns, I don't propose to send you on a guilt trip; I want to help you understand yourself and examine your way of functioning.

JESUS SAID...

Scripture Verses

"Therefore, there is now no condemnation for those who are in Christ Jesus."

—Romans 8:1

PATTERNS RUN DEEP *continued . . .*

Read the verse from Romans in the margin. How do you feel when you read this promise from God's Word about what has gone before? Below check all answers that apply.

❑ My financial wrongdoings are so great, I don't see how it's possible that the Father isn't condemning me.

❑ I want to believe that the slate is wiped clean when I ask forgiveness, but guilt over my financial sins weighs me down.

❑ God's Word is true. Even though I feel sad about my wrong choices in the past, I understand God's promise that I am condemned no more.

❑ I will try to look on the examination of my past failures — or past harmful influences regarding debt — as God-given, not to blame but to bring godly insight so I can succeed in the future.

Based on this exercise, voice a prayer to God, asking for His ability to help your unbelief and to give you a clear mind to examine past patterns.

List at least one pattern — positive or negative — that you see in your life today. Describe how this pattern affects the way you manage money.

_____

_____

_____

_____

_____

_____

Week 2, Day 1

Notes

JESUS SAID...

LOOKING AT SYMPTOMS

This Week

Scripture Verses

The symptoms I see when I counsel with financially troubled families are distressingly predictable. The same basic errors in early family training occur throughout society. Many young couples today are from families with nice homes, two cars, color television sets, and a variety of credit sources used to purchase them. Their parents don't operate on a budget and consequently don't train their children to do so. Parents use credit readily and make buying decisions based on the amount of monthly payments rather than on the actual price of the item (initial costs plus interest). Families provide children with credit cards to buy clothes for themselves and gas for their cars. Most of those families dissolve over debt-related problems, but usually the children are sheltered from the circumstances and never make the connection.

Once married and on their own, a young couple attempts to duplicate in three years what may have taken their parents twenty years to accumulate. The results are predictable: within three years they have a lot of things, but these assets are all tied up in debts.

Do you know families like those I just described? If so, go back and underline descriptions that remind you of others — or of yourself.

Let's look at the first two of the four symptoms we see most often in financial distress situations:

Symptom 1: They can't pay monthly bills.
Once the maximum limits have been reached on credit cards and other readily available credit sources, pressures begin building. Creditors begin to harass. Each month, things worsen. Finally, in desperation, a bill consolidation loan is made. That lowers the overall monthly payments and stretches the debt out for a longer period of time. The person or family resolves to avoid the credit trap, and the pressure eases. Within a year the small debts return (the consolidation loan eats up all the available surplus), and the situation is worse than before.

"A prudent man sees danger and takes refuge, but the simple keep going and suffer for it."
—Proverbs 22:3

Read the verse in the margin. How would this message from God's Word apply to an individual in the situation described above? (Answer in space provided on next page.)

Week 2, Day 2

_____
_____
_____
_____
_____
_____

A person with this symptom keeps going — keeps getting further in debt — because he or she did not make changes in the use of credit; therefore, the debt cycle repeats itself.

Symptom 2: More income is needed.

That conclusion seems logical at the time because such persons have already tried a consolidation loan, and more credit can't be the answer. So, usually the wife goes to work outside the home. If the family has small children, involving child care, the result may be a break-even situation or worse. Where no children are involved, the end result is more money in and more money spent. Often, within a year or less, the bills are larger rather than smaller, and the pressures are even greater, because now the extra income is necessary.

Read Proverbs 29:18 at right. How would applying God's Word help people who are tempted to cast off restraint as they acquire more income?

"Where there is no revelation, the people cast off restraint; but blessed is he who keeps the law."
—Proverbs 29:18

_____
_____
_____
_____

You might have replied that God's Word reminds individuals about the hazards of debt and is intended to help them see how God expects them to spend their money responsibly, therefore stopping harmful patterns of spending and borrowing.

JESUS SAID...

Week 2, Day 2

LOOKING AT SYMPTOMS *continued . . .*

Based on the two practical assignments you've been working on since this course began, do you recognize either of these two symptoms as you study your personal income, outflow, and outstanding debt? If so, describe how these descriptions apply to you.

_____

_____

_____

_____

As you pray to wrap up today's work, consider completing these sentences as prayer-starters:

- Lord, I already recognize that I've not kept Your commands by . . . .
- Please give me the courage and insight to help me . . . .
- Thank You that You're already showing me how to . . . .

Week 2, Day 2

Notes

JESUS SAID...

Week 2, Day 3

THE PRESSURE INTENSIFIES

Scripture Verses

"A man of great anger shall bear the penalty, for if you rescue him, you will only have to do it again."

—*Proverbs 19:19*

The other two symptoms I see frequently in counseling financially distressed persons are equally potent.

Symptom 3: Can't stand the pressure? Buy something new.
Usually, after a time the financed car and washing machine break down, the house begins to need some repairs, and marital pressures reach a boiling point. The logical answer seems to be to buy a new car or take a vacation to "get away from it all." Unfortunately, things seem to worsen, and, as desperation sets in, people solicit loans from family and friends. Many well-meaning Christians get involved with bail-out programs at this point. They think they're helping the situation and cannot see they're only dealing with the symptoms rather than the problems.

Read the verse in the margin. Are you a person who gets "leaned on" by a desperate friend or relative? Or have you found yourself sending the SOS out to others? Describe your answers to these two questions.

_____

_____

_____

_____

Rescuing someone doesn't allow that person to learn on his or her own. After all, the day may come when there is no friend or relative who will bail you out! Will the person have learned skills to meet his or her own needs at that point? Again, this admonition applies both to the rescuer and rescuee. If you are the one always appealing for help, how will you ever learn to stand on your own two feet if you constantly rely on someone's aid?

Symptom 4: Divorce or Bankruptcy.
Once financial pressures build, marital pressures build as well. Communication between spouses is difficult when problems are the only topics of their conversations. The wife may feel insecure, and the husband may become defensive. For a few families, bankruptcy seems to

Week 2, Day 3

be the solution, so they liquidate their debts and begin again. Since credit is easily obtained, they have no difficulty in borrowing again. Shortly, many of these couples will face the same symptoms that promoted the first bankruptcy. (In your Week 5 work, you'll read more about bankruptcy as an option.)

Those who choose divorce find that the same symptoms appear in their next marriage. Some recognize this and seek immediate help. Many don't, however, and eventually find second and third marriages ruined by the lack of a sound spiritual and financial foundation.

It hurts to realize that these symptoms recur in the non-Christian community. Even worse, the same symptoms occur within Christian families and at about the same ratio. If we Christians were truly living by sound biblical principles, our lives would be lights to attract those who desperately need help. Our crises can be traced back to not teaching or applying the basic biblical principles God has established in His Word. Some principles are so fundamental, it would seem all Christians would understand them. Unfortunately, they don't.

What are some biblical principles you can recall? Below jot down two or three verses that come to mind that are good guides for couples or individuals regarding financial responsibility.

_____

_____

_____

You might have mentioned some verses such as Proverbs 3:9-10, Proverbs 6:6-8, Matthew 6:24, or Hebrews 13:5.

Take one of these verses and pray it as a prayer back to God. For example, if you named Hebrews 13:5, you might say, "Lord, help me to be content with what I have and to keep my life free from an obsession to spend money on things."

JESUS SAID...

ATTITUDES THAT HURT

Scripture Verses

"The wicked borrows and does not pay back, But the righteous is gracious and gives."
—*Psalm 37:21*

"Let no debt remain outstanding, except the continuing debt to love one another."
—*Romans 13:8*

S ome harmful **attitudes** about money also form a common thread that runs through the marriages and families of those in financial distress. If you're trying to answer the question, "How did I get this way?" see if one of these attitudes applies to you.

Harmful Attitude #1: Borrowing is "normal."

Scripture clearly indicates that borrowing is not normal to God's plan and was never intended to be used as a routine part of our financial planning. Logically, it should be limited to appreciating assets, thus avoiding "surety."

Read the first two verses appearing in the margin. Below describe what the Scripture says about borrowing.

_____

_____

_____

_____

Scripture says, "Repay what is owed." It further says that our allegiance should not be to a creditor but to the love of others, because of Christ's love. Children should be encouraged to save for needs, not to borrow to get them. Parental examples of trusting God to provide without borrowing are woefully lacking today.

Harmful Attitude #2: Saving is "abnormal."

In our upside-down inflationary economy, spending and borrowing are promoted as logical. Saving is discouraged — and even penalized. I assure you that those who borrow and spend always look for a saver in time of crises. Children should be taught that it is more sound, biblically and financially, to save for future needs than to rely on creditors. It's a sad indictment of how far we have strayed from God's truth when the average 65-year-old man today has accumulated less than $100 in free and clear assets [Social Security Administration phone number/Internet address: 1-800-772-1213 — www.ssa.gov].

Week 2, Day 4

Scripture Verses

In the verse at right, underline the word used to describe the *saver* and the word used to describe the *spender*.

You probably answered that the saver, who has accumulated what he needs for the future, is described as *wise,* while the man who spends it all in his greed is *foolish.*

Harmful Attitude #3: Hasty decisions are not necessarily harmful.
Patience and consistency, rather than quick decisions and instant success, are the ways to financial security. People can build a firm financial foundation by taking small steps over a long period of time. They also can remember that God's plan is not the same for everyone. Children are not promised automatic affluence just because their parents have it. One of the best disciplines a parent can teach a child is to allow him or her to work to reach a goal. Too often everything is given without any effort on the child's part. This can create a lifetime habit of expecting something for nothing.

Read Proverbs 21:5 in the margin. Below describe a time in which you have reached a goal (financial or otherwise) by diligence and patience (rather than by acting hastily).

_____

_____

_____

_____

Harmful Attitude #4: Budgeting is not important.
People can learn to live on a reasonable budget. Parents can leave no greater financial asset to their children than the knowledge of how to establish and live on a balanced budget. Over-spending should be so discouraged in Christian homes that children wouldn't even consider it a possibility in their own homes later. Remember, at best, the tug of worldly ways will tempt them down the wrong paths. At worst, our failure to train will send them down those paths without a way back.

"In the house of the wise are stores of choice food and oil, but a foolish man devours all he has."
—Proverbs 21:20

"The plans of the diligent lead to profit as surely as haste leads to poverty."
—Proverbs 21:5

39

JESUS SAID...

ATTITUDES THAT HURT *continued . . .*

Scripture Verses

"He who ignores discipline comes to poverty and shame, but whoever heeds correction is honored."
—*Proverbs 13:18*

Read the verse at left. Below describe one thing you learned about budgets during your growing-up years at home.

_____
_____
_____
_____

Based on the two practical assignments you've been working on since the introduction to this course, — (1) identifying every outstanding debt you have and (2) accounting for 100 percent of your take-home income — do you recognize any of these four *attitudes* influencing you as you earn, spend, borrow, or pay creditors? If so, go back and put a star beside any of the areas in which you believe you need to work on improved attitudes.

Ask a prayer partner (someone besides your spouse) to pray that God will help you to set aside harmful attitudes that apply to you.

Write down one thing Jesus has said to you through the verses you have studied this week.

_____
_____
_____
_____

Week 2, Day 4

Notes

JESUS SAID...

LIVING BY THE WORD

Examine these case studies of people who struggle with harmful attitudes and with deep-seated symptoms of financial distress. State how the person would respond if he or she were trying to live by sound biblical principles concerning money.

Trevor's dad had been irresponsible with bills. Because his parental role model was poor, Trevor had trouble, as an adult, saying "No" to his children. Soon credit-card bills overwhelmed the family. When his wife asked him to draw the line, he found that he didn't have the will or the training to control his finances.

_____

_____

_____

_____

Maxie spent her lunch hours shopping at the department store near her office. She ran up large credit-card bills — more than she could pay at the end of the month. Maxie assumed that it was okay as long as she could make the payments each month.

_____

_____

_____

_____

Clyde struggled to make monthly house payments and sometimes got behind. He also was still paying on a student loan. He saw a car he wanted and begged his dad to cosign a loan with him, since his credit wasn't good enough to borrow on his own.

_____

_____

_____

_____

Week 2, Day 5

Carla enjoyed gardening and wanted to buy bedding plants for her yard. She was trying to pay off some debts and was curtailing expenditures, but she rationalized that she could charge the items since the discount sale would be more than the interest she would pay.

_____
_____
_____
_____

Trevor should realize that through Christ's salvation, all people are made new. This would keep him from feeling enslaved by his past and would enable him to set healthy standards for himself and his family. Maxie should remember the Bible's admonition to repay what is owed, prompting her to break her habit of unpaid balances that could easily escalate. Clyde should see that leaning on someone for a bail-out plan keeps him from experiencing God's best. Carla could recall the verse in Proverbs about diligence and delay her desire for instant gratification until she had cash to pay for her gardening items.

Below, describe how a premise from this week's work has helped you gain insight as you continue to work on your two practical assignments given you at the start of this course. (See page 8.)

_____
_____
_____
_____
_____
_____
_____
_____

Ask God to help you look for the Truth from His Word anytime you are contemplating a money-related issue.

JESUS SAID...

SEEKING FIRST THINGS FIRST

Scripture Verses

"Let us not become weary in doing good, for at the proper time we will reap a harvest if we do not give up."
—Galatians 6:9

"But seek first His Kingdom and His righteousness; and all these things shall be added to you."
—Matthew 6:33

"If you abide in Me and My words abide in you, ask whatever you wish, and it shall be done for you."
—John 15:7

Congratulations on completing your assignments over the past two weeks! You're beginning to "size up" what's really happening in your family finances. Though this work may seem discouraging or tedious at times, take heart! You're completing difficult tasks leading to financial freedom that will return a lifetime of benefits. See the apostle Paul's words at left.

Now that you have begun to focus on some of the root causes of financial bondage, you can focus on God's plan for financial freedom. Begin by committing your entire financial circumstances to God in prayer. In Weeks 1 and 2 you learned that God genuinely cares about you — yes, you! He wants to be involved with the financial details of your life. You can trust Him to help you carry your burden.

Read the words of Jesus in the margin. If you were to apply this passage to your financial situation, how do you think "seek first His Kingdom and His righteousness" would be reflected in what you are doing? Check all that apply.

❏ 1. Give a tenth of my income to the church.
❏ 2. Scale down my "want list" and determine "How much is enough?" in my life.
❏ 3. Give to support missionaries.
❏ 4. Pay my bills on time.
❏ 5. Pray about how God would have me reduce my financial burdens.

No doubt, God would approve of your taking all of these steps. Perhaps, in time, you'll find yourself accomplishing all these tasks. For now, though, turning these matters over to the Lord in prayer is an ideal "first" way to seek the Kingdom of God and His righteousness first.

A common question about prayer is, "How do I know what kind of prayers God will answer?" Most people genuinely desire to pray as God desires. In John 15:7, appearing in the margin, Jesus gives some guidelines for praying in this way.

Week 3, Day 1

Read John 15:7. Based on this verse, how do you think you should pray about financial matters?

_____

_____

_____

This verse has a wonderful promise in it — but many people read it to mean, "God will give me anything I ask." On close examination, however, John 15:7 says something else entirely. It promises that God will answer your prayers *if* you abide in Him and if His Word abides in you.

How can you abide in Him and have His Word abide in you in the area of finances? Abiding in Christ, or remaining in Him, involves spending time with Him. You can't get to know a potential friend, your life's mate, or a neighbor without spending some time talking with that person. Spending time with the Master is one way to abide in Him, so you'll know what He's trying to say to you.

Do you have a daily quiet time to communicate with God? ❑ Yes ❑ No. If so, write the time and place of your daily quiet time. If not, will you commit today to begin a daily quiet time?

_____

Does God's Word abide in you? Do you spend time in God's Word daily, so that you are already acquainted with Jesus on money — the whole of scriptural precepts regarding your finances? ❑ Yes ❑ No

Will you make it a practice to memorize Scripture so you will have God's Word hidden in your heart, to recall when you need it to help you? ❑ Yes ❑ No

The Father delights to hear you when you pray His Word back to Him and claim His promises. If you don't spend time in His Word, you can't know what He desires for you in the area of money. Therefore prayer is important.

JESUS SAID...

Week 3, Day 1

SEEKING FIRST THINGS FIRST *continued . . .*

Scripture Verses

"But seek first his kingdom and his righteousness, and all these things will be given to you as well."
　　　　—Matthew 6:33

"Do not store up for yourselves treasures on earth, where moth and rust destroy, and where thieves break in and steal."
　　　　—Matthew 6:19

"A greedy man stirs up dissension, but he who trusts in the Lord will prosper."
　　　　—Proverbs 28:25

Give it a try. Read the three verses in the margin. Choose one of these passages from God's Word and use it as the basis of a prayer for your finances.

For example, if you chose the first verse, you might have prayed, "Lord, help me to seek Your will first when it comes to how I spend my money. I claim the promise of Your blessings if I give You first priority."

Will God answer you when you ask for a particular model sports car or a specific label dress? Should you ask for a certain amount of money to come your way so you can pay an overdue bill? No one can limit God, so praying for specifics is not outside the realm of possibility. However, the Bible is clear on one thing: God answers prayers that are prayed according to His will. How can you know what prayers mesh with God's will? Read what Jesus has to say in Matthew 6:25-34.

Set aside a time of commitment about getting your financial circumstances in order. You may do this creatively as a family in a simple worship experience in your own home, or you may do it privately. Before your next group session, plan to devote some time to praying the kinds of prayers about your finances that God will answer.

Below write your plan for your prayer time of commitment.

_____

_____

_____

_____

Week 3, Day 1

Notes

JESUS SAID...

LIVING WITHIN YOUR MEANS

Scripture Verses

"The plans of the diligent lead surely to plenty, But those of everyone who is hasty, surely to poverty."
     —Proverbs. 21:5

"But if we have food and clothing, we will be content with that."
     —1 Timothy 6:8

If you've committed to get out of debt, or want to be sure you never fall into the debt trap in the first place, adopting a budget is necessary. Did you flinch when you read that "B" word? If so, you're not alone. To many people, the word *budgeting* has a bad connotation. These folks liken adopting a budget to marching off to a concentration camp! Actually, it might feel this way to a family attempting to correct in one day the financial problems that took them years to develop. As you assessed your current financial situation in weeks 1 and 2, you probably realized that these difficulties were months, or even years, in the making.

Budgeting does not have to be something formidable. A budget is simply a plan to ensure that you know where your money goes each month. What this book proposes is a simple, workable plan for home money management — one that brings the financial area under God's control and keeps you from worry, frustration, or anger over money. When you maximize family finances, you are more effective for God both spiritually and financially. The budget becomes a tool for good communications in an area normally characterized by conflict.

The goal in budgeting is to live within your means — to spend no more than you make on a monthly basis. If you're constantly spending more money than you earn, you're living beyond the means God has supplied for you. Ideally good budgeting means living on a current basis and not using credit or borrowed money to provide normal living expenses. It also means being disciplined enough to control spending and to keep needs, wants, and desires in balance.

Let's look at these three categories:

Category 1: Needs — These are the items necessary to provide your basic requirements for living. First Timothy 6:8 at left speaks to these needs.

What do you consider to be "needs" for your family?

_____

_____

_____

Week 3, Day 2

You might have listed such items as food, clothing, housing, medical coverage, gasoline, water, or electricity.

Category 2: Wants — Wants involve choices about the quality of goods to be used. The choice may be between dress clothes vs. work clothes, steak vs. hamburger, a new car vs. a used car, a luxurious home vs. a comfortable, adequate home. First Peter 3:3-4 gives a point of reference for determining wants in a Christian life.

Can you think of a time in which you confused a want with a need? If so, describe below.

_____
_____
_____

Most people have fallen into this trap. For example, someone might have written in the blanks above, "I needed a new ballpoint pen. Although my basic need was merely for something with which to write, I got carried away and bought a fancy, gold, luxury-brand pen. I wanted one that was special, and I thought people would be impressed if they saw this recognizable style sticking out of my shirt pocket." Unfortunately, today's culture teaches us to strive to be pampered — that we deserve all the perks we can get our hands on, even if we can't afford them.

Category 3: Desires — These are choices according to God's plan that can be made out of surplus funds only after all other obligations have been met. Read what 1 John 2:15-16 says about this.

Think about one of your desires. Based on the verses you just read, how do you think that desire stacks up in the Father's eyes? Stop and pray about that thing you desire. Ask God to show you what choice He would have you make regarding it.

Most Americans need a car. Clearly, that *need* can be met with a '76 Chevy (for about $500). But I might *want* a new Chevy (for about $20,000). Or I

"Your beauty should not come from outward adornment, such as braided hair and the wearing of gold jewelry and fine clothes. Instead, it should be that of your inner self, the unfading beauty of a gentle and quiet spirit, which is of great worth in God's sight."
　　　　—1 Peter 3:3-4

"Do not love the world or anything in the world. If anyone loves the world, the love of the Father is not in him. For everything in the world — the cravings of sinful man, the lust of his eyes and the boasting of what he has and does — comes not from the Father but from the world."
　　　　—1 John 2:15-16

JESUS SAID...

LIVING WITHIN YOUR MEANS *continued . . .*

Notes

might *desire* a luxurious import (for about $60,000 or more). The function is the same. The esthetics are not.

In last week's work you read about some obstacles — some things that possibly helped you answer the question, "How did I get here?" Some of these were bill-consolidation loans, additional credit, second mortgages, bankruptcy, divorce, or the wife's outside employment. These temporary measures only treat the symptoms, while the problems still exist. In only a matter of time, the symptoms will reappear.

Generally, it's better and faster to cut expenses than to attempt to increase income. Unfortunately, cutting expenses can be painful. The key? Commitment.

List one thing you desire after all present obligations are met, and ask God for His guidance in this desire.

_____

_____

_____

Name one specific way you have demonstrated commitment in your Christian life.

_____

_____

_____

_____

Your answer may have included memorizing Scripture, reading your Bible daily, attending church regularly, keeping God's laws, or remembering to tell others about Jesus.

You can also demonstrate commitment in the financial arena. God will show you how!

Week 3, Day 2

Notes

JESUS SAID...

Week 3, Day 3

RECOGNIZING INCOME DIVISIONS

Whatever your goal — whether it's to get out of debt or to ensure that you never fall into the debt trap in the first place — it helps to look at the basic divisions of your income. These divisions fall into five categories.

1. **The first part belongs to God.** It's the tip of the iceberg — the portion of your income that you return to Him first as a tithe to acknowledge that He owns all that you have. You are merely a steward of those things that have been entrusted to your care. Read Malachi 3:8. The testimony of tithing is that God will bless and enable you to stretch the 90 percent you keep and manage further than if you keep 100 percent for yourself.

2. The **government** wants its share, as Jesus describes in Matthew 22:21b.

3. **Family needs** are next. See what 1 Timothy 5:8 says.

4. God says you are to **pay your debts.** This is mandated in Psalm 37:21.

5. If you are a good steward and manage faithfully, your labor will yield a **surplus.** The surplus allows you, as a Christian, to respond to others' needs. See 2 Corinthians 8:14. Besides enabling you to share with others, the surplus keeps you prepared for emergencies so you don't have to use credit. You also can invest your surplus to multiply your assets.

Based on the work you've already completed on your income and outgo chart, how do you feel you stack up in these categories? Go back and put a star by the area in which you struggle most.

If you're like most people, you find that you fall short in keeping these divisions in balance — especially in the area of having a surplus. The solution to this is maintaining a budget. Do you ever look at a map and immediately try to find the big red dot that pinpoints, "You are here" before you set out on your destination? Setting a course is difficult without first determining where you are. Budgeting is a two-step process:

This Week

Day 1:   Seeking First Things First
Day 2:   Living Within Your Means
Day 3:   Recognizing Income Divisions
Day 4:   Budget Problem Areas
Day 5:   The Guideline Budget

Scripture Verses

"Will a man rob God? Yet you are robbing Me! But you say, 'How have we robbed Thee?' In tithes and offerings."   —Malachi 3:8

"Then He said to them, 'Then render to Caesar the things that are Caesar's; and to God the things that are God's.'"   —Matthew 22:21b

"But if anyone does not provide for his own, and especially for those of his household, he has denied the faith, and is worse than an unbeliever." —1 Timothy 5:8

"The wicked borrows and does not pay back, But the righteous is gracious and gives."   —Psalm 37:21

"At the present time your plenty will supply what they need, so that in turn their plenty will supply what you need. Then there will be equality."
                —2 Corinthians 8:14

Week 3, Day 3

1. **Step One — What is the present level of spending?** That's what you've been doing with your two practical assignments.

2. **Step Two — Budget goals: establishing the "ideal" budget.** Few people ever reach the ideal. But how can you succeed if you never have a goal? As you establish your budget, you'll contrast your present spending level with a guideline for balanced spending. The comparison will point out where you need to make adjustments. You'll also put in place a control system that will keep spending on the "road." The system is designed to sound the alarm before overspending occurs. You'll study this "how to stay out of debt" aspect in your Week 6 work.

As you establish your budget, you'll run into road hazards. Let's look at three of these road *hazards*.

Hazard #1: Discouragement
Discouragement will easily occur. To complete the trip you must keep going. Many people develop a budget but then fail to follow it.

Describe a time in the past when you may have become discouraged because you strayed away from a budget you had set.

_____

_____

_____

_____

_____

_____

Hazard #2: Legalism and inflexibility
The budget can easily become a family weapon instead of a family tool. Becoming legalistic, incidentally, seems to occur at the same time the money runs out. If a road is blocked, you may have to take another route to get where you are going. Remain flexible so that you can make necessary changes.

JESUS SAID...

RECOGNIZING INCOME DIVISIONS *continued . . .*

Scripture Verses

Hazard #3: Overcorrection

When the money gets tight, the tendency is to eliminate clothes, entertainment, food, and other discretionary items. This, in turn, creates a pressure that often causes people to overspend in other areas. One particular family with whom I counseled wrestled with how to chart a new financial course in their lives and make necessary corrections. A few of their stories are included in this study, with their permission. Here's how they dealt with this particular area:

When it came time for Homecoming weekend at the high school, no money was left for Annie to buy the dress she wanted. "You'll have to wear something you already have," her father growled. Later he felt guilty and said, "Here, take my credit card and have a good dinner before the dance." Annie did just that, taking two friends with her. It resulted in a sizeable credit-card bill, which led to a big argument.

Has this scene — or one similar to it — ever happened in your family because of overcorrection? If so, describe below.

_____
_____
_____
_____
_____
_____
_____
_____

"Who then is the faithful and wise servant, whom the master has put in charge of the servants in his household to give them their food at the proper time?"
—*Matthew 24:45*

Financial bondage can result from a lack of money and overspending, but it also can arise from the misuse of an abundance of money. Some families have enough money to be undisciplined and get away with it, financially speaking. But even in their excesses, are these people truly financially free? True financial freedom requires that you be a good steward, as Jesus illustrates in Matthew 24 at left. That is only possible with self-discipline.

Week 3, Day 3

Be aware. Satan will try to trip you up in this process. He will use debt or any one of an endless array of devices to try to convince you that you can't conquer your finances. Satan hates to see anyone trying to follow God's commands. He will use circumstances to discourage you, so that you can't regain control of your family budget. See the verse at right.

A good plan requires action and discipline to make it work. It may require sacrifice. Delay accomplishes nothing but only puts off the inevitable. Begin now!

So you won't feel discouraged as you commit your finances to the Lord, ask God to help you overcome negative self-talk and to focus on His truths.

Considering where you are financially today, what do you believe Jesus is saying to you through Matthew 24:45 and 1 Peter 5:8-9?

_____
_____
_____
_____
_____
_____
_____
_____

Scripture Verses

"Be self-controlled and alert. Your enemy the devil prowls around like a roaring lion looking for someone to devour. Resist him, standing firm in the faith . . . ."
—1 Peter 5:8-9

JESUS SAID...

This Week

Scripture Verses

"Whoever can be trusted with very little can also be trusted with much, and whoever is dishonest with very little will also be dishonest with much."
—*Luke 16:10*

BUDGET PROBLEM AREAS

One of your two practical assignments involved determining your present spending level (where you are). I hope the guides I have included with the Monthly Income and Expenses worksheet have helped you gather this material (see pages 120-121). From this point on in your work, you'll be learning how to make mid-course corrections. Tomorrow, you'll learn about a guideline budget, which divides family spending into percentages to help determine the proper balance in each category of the budget. That will help you get from where you are to where you want to be — a new budget that deals with the areas of overspending.

Before we do that, let's look at four *problems* that can wreck your budget. These include:

- bookkeeping errors
- impulse buying
- gifts
- hidden debts

Problem Area #1: Bookkeeping Errors
Keep your checkbook accurately balanced and current. Even small errors, if allowed to compound, grow into big problems. An inaccurate balance can result in an overdrawn account, as well as in significant bank charges. Such work may seem tedious at times, but remember what Jesus says (see Scripture at left) about the person who is faithful in little things.

Automatic banking systems create additional pitfalls. Remember to subtract automatic payment deductions from the checkbook ledger at the time the bank pays them.

For example, you may arrange for your utility bill to be paid by automatic withdrawal on the fifteenth of each month. Since no statement or notice arrives from the electric company, make certain that on the fifteenth of every month, you deduct the proper amount from your home checking-account records. The same thing applies to automatic credit card payments, insurance premiums, or any other automatic withdrawal.

Week 3, Day 4

Money machines are convenient, but they can also lead to inaccuracies. If you use an automatic teller machine (ATM) to withdraw cash from your account, be sure you note this withdrawal in your ledger immediately and file the transaction record.

Other points to consider:

- A ledger-type checkbook with duplicate checks, rather than a stub type, gives greater visibility and lends itself to fewer errors. Have you ever tried one of these? ❑ Yes ❑ No

- Make certain all checks are accounted for.

- Each family needs only one bookkeeper. The choice should be based on who can do the job best. Who in your family is best at this?

  _____

- Maintain a Home Ledger (See page 125). If you keep all records in a checkbook ledger, you run the risk of losing it. A home ledger eliminates this possibility and makes record-keeping more orderly. Have you ever tried this system? ❑ Yes ❑ No

- Balance the account every month, to the penny. The two most common errors are arithmetic errors and transposition errors (writing in the wrong amount, i.e. $98.95 instead of $89.95). Use a calculator.

- Consider a software program to use on your home computer such as Snap-Shot Gold (0-6330-0925-3 – Available from LifeWay, 1-800-458-2772).

**How would you rate your ability to keep checkbook balances current?
Go back and put a star by the area or areas in which you need to work.**

Problem Area #2: Hidden Debts or Expenses

People commonly overlook non-monthly expenses such as doctor bills, family loans, quarterly insurance premiums, or bank notes. This leaves no budget allocation for them when they come due. Maintaining a list of expenses in total, such as the one you have been working on in this book, will help avoid surprises (see Introduction page 8). The budget must anticipate necessary payments. See the verse at right regarding debt.

"Let no debt remain outstanding, except the continuing debt to love one another, for he who loves his fellowman has fulfilled the law."
—*Romans 13:8*

JESUS SAID...

BUDGET PROBLEM AREAS *continued . . .*

Scripture Verses

"In the house of the wise are stores of choice food and oil, but a foolish man devours all he has."
—*Proverbs 21:20*

Problem Area #3: Gifts
Overspending on gifts is a major budget-buster in most families. Unfortunately the net result is often a gift someone doesn't want, purchased with money that was needed for something else. Sometimes costs go up because the person selects the gift at the last minute. If gifts are part of normal spending, budget for them and buy ahead, reasonably.

A good plan is to keep an event calendar for the year and budget ahead. One good family rule: no gifts are to be bought on credit. Watch for sales and shop from catalogs to get the best price on gifts. Shop for Christmas gifts all year long. Having everything bought before the holidays also greatly reduces stress during the year's busiest time. The verse at left illustrates this kind of prudence.

Problem Area #4: Impulse Buying
Impulse buys are unnecessary purchases made on the spur of the moment. You may rationalize these purchases by saying, "It was on sale," or "I've worked hard all week. I deserve this." Impulse buys may be small items or big purchases like homes, cars, trips, and unscheduled luncheons. Often people pay for them with credit cards because cash isn't available. The net result is an unwise purchase and an unnecessary debt.

Can you describe a time you succumbed to an impulse-buying urge? What resulted?

_____

_____

_____

_____

Consider every purchase in light of your budget. Discipline is the key to controlling the impulse-buying urge. Pledge to yourself that instead of buying on impulse, you will wait three days (30 days for big items) before purchasing the item and during that time get at least two additional prices. At the end of that time, if you have available cash and still need the item, buy it. This is a useful practice to end impulse-buying.

Week 3, Day 4

Read the verse appearing at right. Think about a time in which you exercised self-control in the area of impulse buying. Stop and thank God that He gave you the strength to resist.

If you have mastered all of these budget problem areas, think back over your life and name events or people that helped influence your positive spending and managing habits.

_____

_____

_____

_____

JESUS SAID...

THE GUIDELINE BUDGET

tudy the Percentage Guide for Family Income (page 124), which represents the whole of family spending divided into recommended percentages to help determine the proper balance for each budget category. Although it is not an absolute, it may help you identify problem areas in your own spending. Percentages are based on a family of four people with incomes ranging from $25,000 or less to $115,000 a year. Above or below those limits, percentages may change, according to family situations and needs. If you are in a lower-income level, basic family needs will dominate your income distribution.

The guideline presents a standard against which you can compare your present spending patterns. It helps you spot areas of overspending that create the greatest patterns. Additionally, it helps you determine where you need to make adjustments. If you are overspending, you can use the percentage guideline as a goal for budgeting. Although the percentages are goals only, they do help establish upper levels of spending.

For instance: If you are spending 40 percent or more of your Net Spendable Income on housing, you will have difficulty balancing a budget. Most family incomes cannot absorb excessive spending on housing.

As you have analyzed your spending patterns during these first weeks of work, have you determined that excess housing costs make it impossible to balance your budget? ❏ Yes ❏ No   **Describe how overspending in one area impacts other areas of your budget.**

_____

_____

_____

_____

Subtract your Tithe and Taxes from your *gross income* to determine your Net Spendable Income. Use the Net Spendable Income to calculate the ideal spending for each budget category. If you know what you pay in taxes, then

Week 3, Day 5

use actual amounts. For example, a family of four with an income of $25,000 a year would pay about 5.1 percent of gross income in taxes (which would qualify them for earned income credit — a special tax benefit for lower-income families). (A single person making $12,000 per year will have a 16 percent tax burden — including 2 percent state tax — based on the standard deduction.) In the example the guideline shows, the Net Spendable Income is $1,768 per month. Thus for housing, spend no more than $672 per month, or 38 percent of the Net Spendable Income. Housing expense includes payment, taxes, insurance, utilities, and upkeep.

Note that in some categories, absolutes are impossible with variables such as utilities and taxes. You must adjust percentages within ranges under Housing, Food and Auto. Those three together cannot exceed 65 percent. Example: if you use 40 percent for Housing, you must reduce the percentages for Food and Auto.

You're into some tough work now. Looking at these guidelines and then comparing them to your actual budget, which you'll do in Week 4, may make you a bit uncomfortable. Introspection is often uncomfortable, especially at first. I promise that you will soon see the fruits of your labor and that God will bless any sincere, thorough efforts you make to chart a better course.

Stop again and commit these plans to the Lord. You may want to make the verse that appears in the margin part of your prayer.

Write down at least one thing you believe Jesus is leading you to do regarding your present spending levels.

"Commit to the Lord whatever you do, and your plans will succeed."
—Proverbs 16:3

_____

_____

_____

_____

JESUS SAID...

THE FORK IN THE ROAD

This Week

Scripture Verses

"Although the Lord gives you the bread of adversity and the water of affliction, your teachers will be hidden no more; with your own eyes you will see them. Whether you turn to the right or to the left, your ears will hear a voice behind you, saying 'This is the way; walk in it.'"
—*Isaiah 30:20-21*

Y ou're into some heavy lifting now — taking some critical steps to becoming a good steward — God's steward. This week you'll take everything you've learned so far and actually infuse that into a new budget that is tailor-made for you and your family. Help is on the way!

You've already done two things: (1) determined your present spending level (where you are), and (2) reviewed the guideline percentages (where you should be). Now your task is to draft a new budget that deals with any areas of overspending. If you see your percentages are way out of line with the suggested guidelines, where do you start bringing them in line? In a healthy budget, total expenditures cannot exceed the Net Spendable Income. If you have more spendable income than expenses, you can control spending to maximize your surplus. Today we'll look at the actual bottom line; for the rest of the week, we'll study some ways you can get those expenses in hand.

Again, please note: This can be a revealing process. Looking at areas where your spending exceeds the guideline can be stressful. Try to look on it as a learning experience. See it as God's method for showing you how to be the best possible steward. See the assurance at left from His Word.

Take the following steps as you prepare to draft your new budget.

Budgeting Step One: Compare — On the Budget Analysis chart (page 123), compare your existing budget (the totals you came up with on pages 120-121) with the Percentage Guide for Family Income (page 124). Note the difference, plus or minus, in the difference column. A negative notation indicates a deficit; a positive notation indicates a surplus.

Budgeting Step Two: Analyze — After comparing the existing and guideline columns, you can then make decisions about any overspending. You may be able to reduce some areas to compensate for overspending in others. For example, if housing expenditures are more than 38 percent — the recommended guideline — you may need to sacrifice in such areas as Entertainment and Recreation, Miscellaneous, or Automobiles. If debts exceed five (5) percent, the problems are compounded. Help from an outside debt management agency may be necessary. Ultimately, the decision becomes one of where and how to cut back.

Week 4, Day 1

It is not necessary that your new budget fit the guideline budget exactly, *but it is necessary that your new budget not exceed Net Spendable Income.*

At this point good communication between spouses is critical. No one person can make a budget work, because it may involve a family financial sacrifice. Without a willingness to sacrifice and personal discipline, no budget will succeed. We'll spend time in Week 5 on husband-wife communication.

Note the flexibility you gain if your family is not in debt! If you have no debt to retire, the percentage that the guideline recommends for debt retirement is available for your use somewhere else in the budget.

Budgeting Step Three: Adjust — Once you review the total picture, decide where adjustments must be made and spending reduced. You may need to consider a change in housing, automobiles, insurance, or private schools. Your particular situation may be so critical that you must consider selling major items such as your house or a car. These are sobering possibilities, but a genuine crisis may require unusual and dramatic actions, and the freedom from financial bondage will be worth the present sacrifice.

When you decide to make an all-out commitment to debt reduction, the housing allocation may be one of the major lifestyle changes you'll have to make. You might even have to scale down your housing to an adequate and comfortable but much smaller home with less square-footage and a lower monthly payment. This will enable you to pay down other debts and eventually double up on house payments, with the goal of paying off your home mortgage early.

The minimum objective of any budget should be to meet the family's needs without creating any further debt.

Pray with a trusted friend. If you are married, pray with your spouse. Ask the Lord to be your strength and shield (you may even want to pray back to Him the verse at right) as you prepare to make adjustments — some of them even major — to bring your spending in line with your budget. Ask Him to show you what He would have you do to be obedient to Him.

"But you are a shield around me, O Lord; you bestow glory on me and lift up my head."
—Psalm 3:3

JESUS SAID...

This Week

Scripture Verses

"She is like the merchant ships, bringing her food from afar." "She considers a field and buys it; out of her earnings she plants a vineyard."
        —*Proverbs 31:14, 16*

GETTING OUT THE SCISSORS

The trim job is on! Literally. One of the first things I recommend is that couples and individuals stop charging and cut up their credit cards. Credit cards actually aren't the real problem, of course! *Unrestrained spending* with credit cards is the problem. If you keep your credit cards, use them only to purchase budgeted items, be sure your spouse agrees before you purchase something on credit, and pay your credit card bills off entirely at the end of each month. The first time you're unable to pay off your credit card bills, definitely cut them up and don't use them again.

The trim job I'm recommending, however, goes far beyond the use of credit cards. It involves looking at each segment of your budget and determining what stays and what goes.

Let's say your food budget is one area in which you see an excess. You're not alone; most American families buy the wrong kind of food: junk food and/or prepared foods. For example, suppose you find that you are spending 16 percent of your Net Spendable Income on food rather than the recommended 12 percent. What would be required to bring that in line?

In some families, food expenses are one of the most difficult areas to curtail. The following are some tips to help stretch the food dollars.

- Decide on a daily menu first. This keeps grocery shopping from being a hunt-and-find expedition and makes it another step in financial planning.

- Shop with a calculator in hand, but avoid spending your entire food budget. Needs will arise during the week that require extra cash. Stop putting items in the basket when you reach a certain cut-off point. Leave $20 in a "food envelope"* to cover unforeseen food needs or to replenish fresh fruit, such as bananas for family cereal.

* *Some families use a cash-only envelope system to manage their spending. Several envelopes are labeled by category of spending — such as Food, Housing, Clothing, Automobile Expenses — and every payday the budgeted amount of cash is placed in each envelope. When an envelope is empty, no further money may be spent in that category until the next pay period.*

Week 4, Day 2

- Keep a specific, written list rather than relying on impulse buying. Keep a clipboard with a preprinted grocery list chart which names, by categories, your most frequent food items purchased. As needs materialize, circle them for next payday's marketing.

- Familiarize yourself with prices at several stores. For example, you might buy milk at a food store that consistently has the lowest prices on that product; margarine and bread may be cheapest at another store; cheese, eggs, and cereal at yet another. (Just be certain you don't eat up your savings on the gas it takes to go from store to store!)

- Buy generic (house) brands (normally cheaper and just as nutritious) wherever possible; clip newspaper coupons; send off for rebates; watch for advertised specials.

- Avoid prepared foods, such as frozen dinners, pot pies, cakes, and cookies. In buying them, you are paying for labor you can provide.

- Buy in large quantities when possible. A membership in a large discount store makes the per-item cost cheaper. Make certain that "buying in bulk" doesn't translate into "eating in bulk."

- Avoid shopping at convenience stores, except in emergencies, because prices are generally much higher.

- Avoid buying non-grocery items in a grocery supermarket, except on sale. These are normally higher-markup items.

- Take along fabric bags. Some groceries discount the total bill as much as five cents per bag when customers provide their own. Those nickels can add up to dollars quickly. You might keep one fabric bag in each family member's car, so the bag will always be available when you need to stop by the store for an item.

- Avoid buying when hungry, especially if you're a "sugaraholic."

- Check every item as it is being rung up at the store and again when you get home. If you spot an error, speak up immediately.

- Serve health-conscious foods (chicken, fish, fresh fruits and vegetables, etc.). This is generally more economical than buying preprepared

Scripture Verses

"She watches over the affairs of her household and does not eat the bread of idleness. Her children arise and call her blessed; her husband also, and he praises her."

–Proverbs 31:27-28

JESUS SAID...

GETTING OUT THE SCISSORS *continued . . .*

Scripture Verses

"Do you not know that your body is a temple of the Holy Spirit, who is in you, whom you have received from God? You are not your own; you were bought at a price. Therefore honor God with your body."
     —1 Corinthians 6:19

processed food items that often are high in fat, sodium, and other harmful substances. Remember the verse at left. When you shop "healthy," you're not only being a good steward of your resources but also of your body, the Holy Spirit's temple.

- Cook in bulk. Prepare multiple meals at one time and freeze portions for future use. (See *Dinner's in the Freezer* by Jill Bond for suggestions.)

Put a star by tips that your family uses already. Write below a couple of other suggestions that you are willing to try to reduce your food budget.

_____
_____
_____
_____
_____

After a few weeks of staying within your food budget limit by shopping wisely and using other cost-cutting measures, you'll feel confident that you can extend this discipline to other areas.

Remember to thank God for enabling you to set good boundaries with your food budget, as well as other areas. You're not taking these steps on your own power but through Him who gives you strength (Philippians 4:13).

"I can do everything through him who gives me strength."
     —Philippians 4:13

Week 4, Day 2

Notes

JESUS SAID...

Week 4, Day 3

WHAT YOU WILL WEAR

Scripture Verses

"Therefore I tell you, do not worry about your life, what you will eat or drink; or about your body, what you will wear. Is not life more important than food, and the body more important than clothes?"
—Matthew 6:25

Jesus didn't include this familiar passage (appearing at left) in the Sermon on the Mount as mere "filler" in a sermon. People in His day, as they do in ours, preoccupied themselves with clothing. Garments for your body, indeed, are necessities of life. But at what point does your concern about what you will wear go beyond necessity and border on obsession? In the clothing area, how much is truly enough? Many Americans, Christians included, cannot distinguish between luxuries and necessities. Consequently, Christians seek fulfillment through the same channels as non-Christians do and then wonder why they have a fruitless Christian walk. It's okay to live comfortably, but many Americans have taken "comfortable" to mean "lavish."

Your budget item for clothing is worthy of attention as you look at ways to bring your actual spending in line with the recommended guideline. If you see an excess, based on the recommended 5 or 6 percent, what can you do to remedy it?

For one family, clothing overspending wasn't just an issue; it was *the* issue. The wife found it hard to say "No" when it came to buying clothing. Two situations resulted: (1) Overspending for clothing purchases killed the rest of the budget. (2) The wife's spending left little or nothing for her husband's or children's needs. She had a one-person budget in a four-person home. After her family prayed for God's guidance with their budget, they began the following strategies for change:

- A cash-only system for clothing (using the envelope system) with cash set aside in the clothing envelope equivalent to the 5 percent budget guideline.

- A family council before each payday, so parents and children could discuss upcoming clothing needs and allocate the money based on whose needs got priority. For example, Dad might be facing an important business meeting for which he needs a new tie, or the daughter might need some casual pants for an upcoming school trip. Each person gets to plead his or her case, and the allocation of money is a group decision.

Week 4, Day 3

Some families use a plan in which every member of the family has a monthly clothing allotment (which can accumulate). As children learn to manage their own clothing budgets, an expensive pair of tennis shoes becomes a serious decision because it affects their other clothing needs and wants.

- Shopping sales, mail-order catalogs, discount houses, consignment shops, factory outlet stores, nearly-new stores, and even yard sales instead of paying top-dollar. Watching for retailers' deep-discount coupons that knock down already-reduced items during end-of-season sales.

- A consistent asking of the question, "How much is enough?" In this family, it might take the form of questions like, "Just how many pairs of earrings do I really need?"or "Why can't I wear last year's swimsuit one more season?"

- Sewing as many clothes as time will allow (average savings of 50-60 percent).

- Educating family members on care of clothing, especially how to launder to preserve clothing items. For example, drying lingerie or knit shirts on a portable drying rack rather than tossing them into a dryer extends the life of these clothing items.

As you did in Day 2, look at the list and put a star by suggestions that your family uses already. What other ideas come to mind that your family might employ to reduce spending in this area?

_____

_____

_____

_____

_____

_____

JESUS SAID...

WHAT YOU WILL WEAR *continued . . .*

Notes

With prudent planning and buying, your family can be clothed neatly and stylishly without great expense. This requires effort as families learn to be good managers of their resources rather than simply consumers.

Pray a prayer similar to this one: "Dear God, help me to make clothing purchases that reflect a need rather than to satisfy my ego. Replace my desire for things with a desire to please You and to use well what You've given me."

As you review what Jesus says in Matthew 6:25, write down how you believe this verse applies to you personally.

_____

_____

_____

_____

_____

_____

_____

_____

Week 4, Day 3

Notes

JESUS SAID...

This Week

Scripture Verses

"On the third day a wedding took place at Cana in Galilee. Jesus' mother was there, and Jesus and his disciples had also been invited to the wedding."

—John 2:1

TWO OTHER SPENDING "HOT SPOTS"

Entertainment, recreation, and school spending represent other budget items that commonly overload a budget. People yield to the "whatever-feels-good" or "guilt-trip" habit of cash allocation in these areas rather than seriously and meticulously planning for expenditures. Those who are in debt cannot use their creditor's money to entertain themselves. The normal tendency is to escape problems, if only for a short while, even if the problems become more acute. Christians must resist that urge and control recreation and entertainment expenses while in debt.

Don't completely eliminate spending for leisure activities! The stress that results is counterproductive to your home and family. Everyone needs a break from the routine. In His well-balanced life, Jesus certainly took time for leisure. (See Scripture at left.) But if you're looking for ways to reduce spending, especially until debts are paid, this is one category in which cutbacks can be made.

A family can allocate a modest amount each month for their entertainment and recreation envelope and a monthly cash supply for their eat-out envelope. Here are some tips.

1. Wait for popular, suitable movies to be released on video rather than paying the more expensive movie theater rates. If you determine that some new release is an absolute "must-see," attend an afternoon matinee at reduced rates.

2. When renting videos, capitalize on the early-return bonus or use two-for-one rental coupons. Returning video cassettes on time to avoid late fees is a must!

3. Buy entertainment discount books, which are available in most major cities of the U.S. These discount coupons offer two-for-one movie and museum admissions and two-for-one restaurant dining (as well as half-price dry cleaning coupons and a host of other values.) When determining a place where the family could eat out, choose a restaurant where these discounts exist rather than acting on a whim.

4. Prepare as many meals as possible at home. Restaurant and fast-food dining need not be eliminated but should be managed carefully so that it

Week 4, Day 4

does not become an automatic option. A chance to dine out becomes a more special experience when it is less routine.

5. Play family games in place of paid entertainment (like some of those unused games received for Christmas!).

6. Plan vacations during "off season" if possible. Consider a camping vacation to avoid motel and food expenses. If flying, use the least expensive coach fare (late night or early morning usually saves 10-20 percent) and book your trip early.

In planning your recreation, consider your example to others. Ask yourself whether the activity honors Christ. Read the verse appearing at right. Below describe a time when your choice of recreational pursuits was not the best witness.

_____
_____
_____
_____
_____
_____

"Whether, then, you eat or drink or whatever you do, do all to the glory of God."
—1 Corinthians 10:31

When plotting out school expenses, an envelope containing school money also helps. When money for a field trip is due or three, new, spiral notebooks are needed right away, having immediate cash, already budgeted, will be a major relief. As most families can attest, school expenses don't end with the standard fees that are routinely charged at the first of the year. School supplies run out, special projects are assigned, extracurricular dues are assessed, and private lessons or tutoring is needed. Planning ahead is a big help.

You might set aside $60 a month for school allocations. Any amount not spent that month can carry over to the next. Any accumulated surplus may offset larger-ticket items, such as uniforms or school trips. However, if more funds than were budgeted were actually needed for school expenses, other categories will have to be adjusted accordingly.

JESUS SAID...

TWO OTHER SPENDING "HOT SPOTS" *continued . .*

Notes

Sometimes group sacrifices must be made when children have school needs. For example, the family I mentioned earlier (in Week 3) rallied behind Annie when her choral group at school was invited to go overseas for a choir trip. They shared with Annie the fun of earning her own way, as she participated in fund-raising efforts, contacted businesses, friends, and other supporters for donations. (When children learn that they must earn some of their wants and desires, it's amazing how quickly they adjust their expenses and activities.) Beyond that, other family members willingly cut back clothing and recreational expenses while Annie was raising money for her trip. They made these cuts instead of borrowing or using credit.

Pat yourself on the back a little. You have good ideas, too! Below, write down one strategy you already use to manage entertainment costs and one way you feel successful in meeting school expenses.

_____

_____

_____

_____

In the past three days you've looked at specific budget strategies in four areas: groceries, clothing, entertainment/recreation, and school. Choose one of those areas, and describe how money for this area was dealt with in the family in which you grew up. Then describe in what way you aspire to follow or differ from that method.

_____

_____

_____

_____

After thinking about this, do you need to stop and thank someone? Perhaps this study has reminded you about something important a family member taught you about money. If so, consider calling that person or sending him or her a note of gratitude.

Week 4, Day 4

Take a walk with your spouse, or with a close friend if you're not married. Discuss which of all the items in your Week 4 work so far will be the most difficult for you to correct. It would be good to stop right now and ask God to help you with this area.

If you have already conquered these hot spots, describe how this came about, and be prepared to share your answer with your small group.

_____
_____
_____
_____
_____
_____

JESUS SAID...

Week 4, Day 5

MAKING IT WORK

By now, ideas hopefully are popping about other areas of your budget in which you can make adjustments. Obviously you could devote a day's work to each category, with dozens of tips like those you just read. Since that's not possible, I'll include a potpourri of ideas from other areas before this week concludes.

Housing — Typically, this is one of the largest home budget problems. Many families buy a home they can't afford, motivated by peer pressure or some other pressure. Owning a home is not necessary for everyone. The decision to buy or rent should be based on needs and on financial ability rather than on internal or external pressure. Purchase a home only if the total payments (mortgage, taxes, insurance, and utilities) do not exceed 38 percent of your *net* income. Do not finance a second mortgage for the down payment. If trading for another house, consider whether you *need* or merely *desire* to do so.

Automobile — Few Christians truly seek God's will for the purchase of cars, so they suffer later because of the financial strains placed on family finances. Evaluate your reason for trading for a new car. Are you simply tired of or bored with your present one? Can your present car be repaired without great expense? Is it basically reliable? Do you really *need* a brand new car, or will a used one do? Pay cash if possible. Be willing to accept minor difficulties on a used car to secure substantial price reductions. Perform routine maintenance — oil change, lubrication, tune-up — regularly to preserve the life of your vehicle. (Budget for these expenses.) Use the least-expensive gasoline recommended for your car, and shop around for gas stations with the lowest prices. Shop insurance rates; they vary a lot!

Home Furnishings — Consult a consumer-buying index for best purchase value. Consider repairing (such as refinishing and re-upholstering) and rebuilding used furniture of good quality. Many good fix-it-guides explain how to do this. Shop local garage sales and furniture consignment shops. Shop for discontinued furniture lines. Watch the furniture section in the local classified ads.

Week 4, Day 5

In all areas I've mentioned, as well as in others, the following set of "think-before-you-buy" guidelines have proved to be helpful. As you contemplate any purchase, ask yourself . . .

- Is it really necessary?
- Does it reflect my Christian ethic?
- Is it the best buy?
- Does it add to or detract from the family?
- Does it lose its value quickly?
- Does it require costly upkeep?
- Will my owning this item add to or subtract from the work of God's Kingdom on earth?

Pray about every purchase. Absolutely no purchase is too large or too small to be the subject of prayer. How can you know God's will if you never ask Him?

Complete this sentence: The last purchase I prayed about was . . . .

A Christian in debt must stop any expenditure that is not absolutely essential for living. (See the verse at right.) Look for services around the home that can be done without outside cost. One man set an example by beginning to wash and iron his own shirts instead of sending them out to a professional laundry. This demonstrated to the rest of the family the degree of self-sacrifice he was willing to seek in order to reach the financial goal; other family members began to take matters more seriously as a result. The Scripture at right from Luke speaks of the sacrificial spirit the Bible expects.

Several other resources have detailed "how-to" sections about each of these budget categories we're discussing, as well as others. For more information on specific ways to reduce your budget in these and other categories, read *Your Finances in Changing Times* or a workbook series, *How to Manage Your Money*, available through LifeWay Christian Resources (1-800-458-2772).

"He who loves pleasure will become poor; whoever loves wine and oil will never be rich."
—Proverbs 21:17

"John answered, "The man with two tunics should share with him who has none, and the one who has food should do the same.'"
—Luke 3:11

JESUS SAID...

Week 4, Day 5

MAKING IT WORK *continued . . .*

Notes

You may need to adopt a plan to accelerate debt payoff. What I suggest is to pay all you can on the account that charges the highest rate of interest but has the lowest balance due and make minimum payments on all other accounts. When that one is paid off, close it and roll what you have been paying on it onto the next account with the highest interest and lowest balance. You can eliminate one account at a time until each is paid off and closed.

Whatever plan you choose, it's important that you have a plan. It's not always fun to get out of debt, but remember, it's worth it!

At this point you have the necessary skills to establish your own budget. Only one additional ingredient is necessary: desire. No budget will implement itself. As you have seen, effort and good family communication are necessary for success.

As you have studied the previous days' work, perhaps you have identified ways you need to improve on financial matters. List two of them below.

_____

_____

_____

_____

_____

_____

Living on a budget is not only prudent, but it can be fun. As you have successes in various areas, share them with others.

What is one budget-control idea you've learned that you'd like to share with others?

_____

_____

_____

_____

Week 4, Day 5

You have seen what a budget will do. But keep your expectations within realistic bounds. Don't expect a budget to:

- Solve your immediate problems,
- Force you to use it,
- Take the place of action.

A budget has to be used in order for it to work. You can:

- **Post it in the open.**
  The place I will post my budget is _____ .

- **Set an achievable goal.**
  The date by which I/we will have this budget fully implemented is
  _____ .

- **Establish a set time and day to review it.**
  Here are my/our plans for reviewing the budget (and making necessary adjustments) once I/we have adopted it and it has been in use for a time: _____ .

In your Day 4 work you went on a walk with your spouse or friend. Now go together on a specific prayer-walk to pray for the needs of your home. Go around the outside perimeter of your house, or through each room, dedicating the activities in that room to God's use. For example, in the kitchen, pray for God's wisdom as you look for ways to shop more wisely for groceries or in the garage as you consider how to replace an aging automobile. As you prayer-walk, pray conversationally and with your eyes open, chiming in with prayer as other needs present themselves.

JESUS SAID...

Week 5, Day 1

THE QUESTION OF BANKRUPTCY

At this point someone may be thinking, "There's no hope for our finances. We're in too deep. A budget won't help us now. We owe too many people and can't just fix things with some minor tweaking. We're considering bankruptcy." But is this the proper, scriptural thing to do?

Do you still feel very desperate? Is bankruptcy something you're considering? If so, describe your thoughts below.

_____

_____

_____

_____

Bankruptcy is a very personal matter to the more than 1.4 million Americans who use it each year. About half of all personal bankruptcies are taken by young couples who have borrowed far beyond their ability to pay. They see bankruptcy as the only way out. Financial bondage threatens their marriages and sometimes their health.

I counseled a couple who owed $6,000 in credit-card bills, $11,000 for a previous consolidation loan, and $15,000 for a home loan. "Obviously," the husband said, "another consolidation loan won't help. The only thing that will help us is a fresh start." A friend in their church offered to lend them the money to file for bankruptcy. Their wise pastor knew that bankruptcy would be just another "quick fix" and recommended counseling. A review of their financial history convinced them that history would repeat itself if they didn't face their situation squarely and sacrifice to pay their debts.

The average family filing for bankruptcy owes only about $4,000. However, this amount is usually composed of many small bills — many of them delinquent. They may have the capacity to pay their creditors, but that would require at least two years of financial sacrifice. We are a generation of "quick-fix" addicts, and the idea of sacrifice isn't very appealing, even to Christians.

Week 5, Day 1

As I have mentioned previously, the way you deal with your money is the clearest reflection of your inner convictions. Excessive debts, even bankruptcies, are only the external indicators of previous spiritual decisions. Literally, they represent a person's attitudes being reflected in actions. That is not to indict those who are in debt or who file for bankruptcy; it's only to reflect what Jesus said in the verse appearing in the margin.

A pastor who had a very heavy debt burden was considering filing for bankruptcy. He feared his creditors would obtain judgments or even garnishments against him. "It's not fair that they can attach my salary," he told me. "I won't be able to feed my family." I asked whether they had tricked him into borrowing their money. He responded that they hadn't tricked him. Then I asked him to put himself in the place of the lender. <u>If that lender were in his congregation, would he respond to a salvation message delivered by a pastor who had filed bankruptcy to avoid paying a debt?</u> Second, <u>I asked him to consider what Jesus would do if He were in his position.</u> After all, isn't that what we're instructed to do as Christ's followers? We are to do nothing that would be solely for our own benefit. See the verse in Philippians at right.

If you were the pastor mentioned above, how would you answer the two questions (underlined above) I posed to him? Write your responses below.

_____

_____

_____

_____

This pastor stood up to his burden, asked his creditors to forgive him, and cut up all of his credit cards. He confessed his error before his church and found several kindred spirits in the congregation. Some wagging of tongues occurred, to be sure, but in great part, he experienced healing and understanding.

In prayer, ask Christ to show you what He would do if He were in your position financially.

"He who is faithful in a very little thing is faithful also in much; and he who is unrighteous in a very little thing is unrighteous also in much. If therefore you have not been faithful in the use of unrighteous mammon, who will entrust true riches to you?"
—Luke 16:10-11

"Owe no one anything except to love one another, for he who loves another has fulfilled the law."
—Romans 13:8

"Do not merely look out for your own personal interests, but also for the interests of others."
—Philippians 2:4

JESUS SAID...

NO "EASY-IN, EASY-OUT" PRINCIPLES

Scripture Verses

"The rich rule over the poor, and the borrower is the servant to the lender."

—*Proverbs 22:7*

"When you make a vow to God, do not delay in fulfilling it. He has no pleasure in fools; fulfill your vow. It is better not to vow than to make a vow and not fulfill it."

—*Ecclesiastes 5:4-5*

"The wicked borrow and do not repay, but the righteous give generously."

—*Psalm 37:21*

As you continue to evaluate whether taking extreme measures is for you, remember that the matter of repayment involves the vow you took when you borrowed the money. Many people overlook the principle that a vow is a promise — in the case of borrowing money, promising to repay according to agreed-upon conditions of the loan. Once you reach that agreement, repayment is not an option; it's an *absolute* as far as God is concerned. The rights all fall to the lender, and the borrower literally becomes the lender's servant, as the verse at left specifies.

Has someone ever made a vow, or promise, to you that was not kept? If so, how did you feel when that occurred?

_____

_____

Most people feel hurt and that they have been taken advantage of when people do not live up to a vow. Imagine how God feels when you disappoint Him in this manner.

How do you apply Ecclesiastes 5: 4-5, in the area of bankruptcy? (Read it at left.)

_____

_____

As we represent Jesus before the world, Christians are admonished to consider the consequences of their actions. That's why Scripture teaches so many principles dealing with borrowing and lending and especially with the misuse of credit. But once a Christian borrows, that person has made a vow to repay.

A counselee once asked me, "Would God direct someone to go bankrupt?" Read the verse at left. Based on this verse, how would you answer if this question were posed to you?

_____

_____

Week 5, Day 2

You might have answered in the way I did: for God to direct someone to take bankruptcy would refute His own Word, which says the wicked borrow and do not repay. God does not desire for us to be wicked; He wants us to be righteous.

Here are some other frequently-asked questions about bankruptcy:

Will God forgive you if you declare bankruptcy? God forgives any sin — past, present, and future — if you confess that it is wrong. Bankruptcy is a legal remedy, not a scriptural remedy. Under the pressures of excessive debts, Christians sometimes yield to a quick-fix, but that doesn't make bankruptcy any more scriptural.

Is bankruptcy a biblical principle based on the year of remission discussed in Deuteronomy 15: 1-2? (See verses at right.) According to God's Word, a release of debtors was to occur every seventh year. However, it was the option of the lender, not the borrower, to release debts.

What if you have no alternative? Sometimes, instead of negotiating repayment, a creditor will file judgments against a person and, because the person has no assets, will insist on writing off the debts through bankruptcy. If that happens to you, you are not responsible for what creditors did or did not do, but you are responsible before God for your actions. If someone forces you into bankruptcy, you are legally, but not scripturally, released from the debts. You are still obliged to repay the loans unless the lender releases you from the debt. God will give you the strength to do so.

What about involuntary bankruptcy? (This occurs when several creditors wish to attach all available assets and to force an individual or corporation to liquidate.) Read the Scripture at right and describe how you believe it answers this question.

_____

_____

_____

_____

_____

"At the end of every seven years you must cancel debts. This is how it is to be done: Every creditor shall cancel the loan he has made to his fellow Israelite. He shall not require payment from his fellow Israelite or brother, because the Lord's time for canceling debts has been proclaimed."
    —*Deuteronomy 15:1-2*

"Do not withhold good from those who deserve it, when it is in your power to act."
    —*Proverbs 3:27*

JESUS SAID...

NO "EASY-IN, EASY-OUT" PRINCIPLES *continued . . .*

Scripture Verses

"A good name is more desirable than great riches; to be esteemed is better than silver or gold."

—Proverbs 22:1

A person might contend that since the creditors initiated the action they have settled any and all claims. But, in today's society, this action is often necessary to preempt a debtor from liquidating all assets and spending the money. For a Christian, the obligation to repay according to the original terms still exists.

What about Chapter 13 bankruptcy? In this process, a court determines how much indebtedness an individual can pay and then directs creditors to operate within that plan. I find no biblical reason to bar a Christian from using such a remedy, providing that once a person repays the court-appointed percentage, he or she repays the remaining portion also.

Read Proverbs 22:1 appearing at left. Have you ever had an attack on your good name, either in word or in deed? What was the outcome? As a result of this, how do you feel now when something has the potential to damage your reputation?

_____

_____

_____

_____

_____

_____

_____

The key element in any decision involving a legitimate loan made to a Christian by another person is that your actions honor the Lord. God has no "easy-in, easy-out" principles. You serve a holy and righteous God who desires that all people come to the saving knowledge of Jesus. If any willful action on your part impedes that process in the life of another, it displeases Him. Just try to share your faith with a creditor involved in a bankruptcy, and the true loss will be evident.

Ask God to show you any action on your part in the area of finances that might be a stumbling block to another person.

Week 5, Day 2

Notes

JESUS SAID...

THE TWO-INCOME FAMILY

In your Week 2 work, it was mentioned that the subject of a second income often arises when people think about taking drastic measures in desperate financial situations. People typically view the prospect of generating additional money as an automatic solution. In many cases, that involves a decision of whether a wife and mother becomes employed full time outside the home. What does the Bible say about this? What are the alternatives for Christian families?

People today commonly accept that both spouses must have outside jobs in order to maintain and operate a home. On the surface, that is true. The costs of new homes, cars, food, and clothing are usually beyond the income ability of the average one-wage-earner family, especially with increasing payroll taxes. Currently, the payments on the average new home require more than half of the average primary wage-earner's pay. The logical conclusion, then, is that people need two incomes. The fault with that logic is that it doesn't consider whether the average family needs the average home.

People who look to the Bible for an absolute ironclad answer on whether women should have outside employment search in vain. The Bible is silent on the matter. Nowhere in Scripture does a "Thou shalt" or a "Thou shalt not" appear on this topic. The Bible, in fact, lists examples of women who had professions.

Can you remember who some of these women of the Bible are? List them below.

_____

_____

_____

_____

You might have stated that the New Testament character Lydia was described as a seller of purple and that Priscilla, wife of Aquila, is described in Paul's epistles as a tent-maker, along with her husband. No doubt the exemplary woman of Proverbs 31 is a businesswoman. Some godly women of the Bible clearly are identified by their work.

Week 5, Day 3

Scripture Verses

But the lack of biblical mandate does not automatically mean that a two-income family is right in every situation. The Bible also doesn't admonish against holding one's head in a bucket of water, but doing so has logical consequences to be avoided. While the Bible does not ban the two-paycheck family, it speaks out strongly about some other priorities in the marriage and family, especially when children are involved.

Before you read ahead, do some thinking. Use your hand or a paper to cover up the paragraphs that follow. What do you think are some biblical precepts that apply to the dual-income issue, even though the Bible is specifically silent? What do you think are some related topics on which the Bible does speak? Give your ideas below.

_____

_____

_____

_____

Perhaps you listed some of the following biblical principles.

Biblical Principle #1: Children are to be disciplined.
The mother's role as a teacher of her children is incontestable. She is to be heavily involved in guiding and disciplining them. (See the verse at right.) If both father and mother are weary, frazzled, and distracted because of the fatigue of their daily work routines, can they provide the supervision and training children need?

Biblical Principle #2: Husbands and wives are to be united.
In many homes, husbands and wives do not totally agree on whether or not they should be a two-income family. All too often one spouse relents under an emotional assault to make his or her point. Perhaps the wife wants to stay home but her husband unduly pressures her to go to work outside the home. See what the Bible says (the second and third verses at right) about the potential of such disharmony. This disharmony will eventually undermine the marriage relationship. A decision of such magnitude must be made with both spouses in one accord, after much prayer and seeking God's will.

"She watches over the affairs of her household and does not eat the bread of idleness. Her children arise and call her blessed."
    —Proverbs 31:27-28a

"Better to live in a desert than with a quarrelsome and il-tempered wife."
    —Proverbs 21:19

"Even in laughter the heart may sorrow, And the end of mirth may be grief."
    —Proverbs 14:13

87

JESUS SAID...

THE TWO-INCOME FAMILY *continued . . .*

Scripture Verses

"Now I want you to realize that the head of every man is Christ, and the head of the woman is man, and the head of Christ is God."
—1 Corinthians 11:3

"Wives, submit to your husbands as to the Lord. For the husband is the head of the wife as Christ is the head of the church, his body, of which he is the Savior."
—Ephesians 5:22-23

"The wise woman builds her house, but with her own hands the foolish one tears hers down."
—Proverbs 14:1

Biblical Principle #3: There should be no confusion in authority.
God's Word establishes the husband as the head of the household (see 1 Corinthians 11:3 and Ephesians 5:22-23 at left). When a wife is employed, loyalties between job and family can get confused. For example, what happens when a boss orders an employed woman to work late every night, causing her to miss out on her home responsibilities repeatedly? Some women may also be duped into a feeling of independence that is actually rebellion. See Proverbs 14:1 at left. If a wife senses this happening, she would be well-advised to preserve her family relationship, even if that means quitting her job.

Beyond these scriptural considerations, review these practical principles.

Practical Principle #1: Misplaced priorities are a danger to the family.
Just as many Christian men abandon the important priorities — God and family — because they believe they must be a success "for their families," many women also rationalize the same way. For example, in a counseling session, the mother of two young children justified what she considered to be a perfectly logical position: "Certainly, I'm not able to be with my children as much as I would like, and I know that my husband really doesn't want me to work, but how could we ever buy a car or take a vacation if I didn't work?" In the future, many older women will look back as many older men now do and say, "I wish I had taken the time to be with my family when I had the opportunity."

In your own life, regardless of your present age, have you ever made this statement or voiced this regret? ❏ Yes ❏ No

Practical Principle #2: Two incomes pose financial dangers.
A family may become overly dependent on a second income. Families should establish very specific goals for this income, or two incomes will become a necessity. At least once a year every two-income couple should reevaluate their goals and objectives, particularly how the wife's income is spent. This would be a good time to review the tax implications of the second income. A young couple would be well-advised not to merge the second income into the family budget. If the family relocates to another

Week 5, Day 3

city because of a job change, illness strikes, or the wife decides to cease outside employment to have children, disaster can occur if the budget is dependent on this extra income. Couples should learn to live on one income and use the second income for one-time purchases, such as a car, furniture, or down-payment on a home, on a cash basis only.

Practical Principle #3: Evaluating needs vs. desires is a continuous challenge.

Even if the second income is used for extra comforts, such as those mentioned above, a continual self-analysis is necessary to determine if these "comforts" have become necessities. More money generated often means just more money to spend. See the verses at right.

Can you think of a time that you began to depend on as a necessity an item or expenditure that started out in your life as a luxury or comfort? If so, describe below.

_____

_____

_____

Has your preoccupation with the things of the world ever pulled you away from God and thus from living in fellowship with Him, as the verse in 1 John suggests? If so, describe what happened.

_____

_____

_____

The fact remains, many women *are* employed outside the home. The fact that women make these choices is not the problem. The fact that so many couples *believe that dual incomes are necessities to maintain the family's finances* is the real problem. A family *can* have one income and get along. You can observe the proof of this in the tens of thousands of single-income homes that manage well.

"Do not love the world or anything in the world. If anyone loves the world, the love of the Father is not in him . . . . The world and its desires pass away, but the man who does the will of God lives forever."
—1 John 2:15, 17

JESUS SAID...

THE TWO-INCOME FAMILY *continued . . .*

Notes

It is also a fact that many women today are involuntary heads of households. We, as Christians, can demonstrate Christlikeness by trying to ease the strain that exists when a person bears the load of parenting children alone and struggles with making ends meet. In such situations, I have seen churches provide church-based child care, provide a ministry to help with car care and appliance repair, and offer counseling services on a sliding scale, based on ability to pay. Church members also can be helpful by recycling their used cars for persons in need and providing a benevolence fund for emergencies.

Some couples today are finding creative solutions to some of these issues. Many women see they can perform outside work from home by telecommuting or through part-time jobs they perform while children nap or after hours. In some other homes, dads and moms both operate home offices so that home-maintenance and parenting tasks are shared on a day-to-day basis during typical working hours. Other dual-income couples share home maintenance and child rearing so that the burden does not fall on one spouse all the time. For example, when a child in the home becomes ill and needs to stay home from school, the mother and dad trade off this responsibility — determined by their work schedules and by which of them can most practically set aside jobs that day. Good husband/wife communication is crucial here.

Those creative solutions are helpful, but they do not negate a serious look at the areas just mentioned. The questions couples can ask themselves in this situation remain the same.
1. What is the goal of the second income — needs, or desires? Is our family overly dependent on a second income?
2. Is my responsibility to the biblical mandates listed in today's work being compromised because of the working arrangement in our marriage?
3. Is the marriage relationship being supported or undermined because of this working arrangement?

Think about how today's study speaks to you — whether you are part of a two-income family, considering whether you need to be one, or have a close friend or family member who is. What kinds of decisions, life-change, or support for others, might today's work prompt you to make? Pray about this.

Week 5, Day 3

Notes

JESUS SAID...

Week 5, Day 4

HUSBAND-WIFE COMMUNICATIONS

Scripture Verses

"For this reason a man will leave his father and mother and be united to his wife, and they will become one flesh."
        —Genesis 2:24

Another thought may have entered your head more than once, especially when you read an exercise in this study that begins with the words, "Discuss with your spouse . . . " or "Think about how you and your spouse decide . . . " If you are married, you may think to yourself: "Talk with my spouse about money? That'll be the day. Money is the great unmentionable topic in our family."

If that's the case, don't feel alone. Most married couples attest to the fact that subjects like child-rearing, food, movies — even sex — are talked about far more in their families than are finances. This occurs because couples, by and large, lack communication skills in the first place.

A marriage is like the partnership of the left and right hands of the same person — matched but totally opposite. God's Word says that two people become one; this goes beyond physical union.

Understanding this truth can greatly enhance a marriage, because it virtually eliminates any idea that one person is subservient to another. Husband and wife are merely different for the purpose of accomplishing various functions. One hand working alone will not accomplish half as much as will two. It would seem opposites do attract. One spouse will get up early, while the other stays in bed. One is punctual; the other is often late. An old cliché is very true: "If husband and wife are identical, one of them is unnecessary."

If you are married, how is this true for you? In what ways are you and your spouse opposites? If you are not married, how does this apply to your parents?

_____

_____

_____

Unfortunately, in any relationship, a balance is difficult to reach. Usually one personality will overwhelm the other, and a marriage will take on a one-sided tilt. More often than not, where finances are concerned, the husband makes all decisions, although in some families, the wife takes on this responsibility.

Week 5, Day 4

How is this job accomplished in your marriage? Which spouse takes on the bulk of the financial tasks? (If you are single, how did this apply in your parents' marriage?)

_____

_____

_____

How did you (or they) make this determination? Check any of the answers below that apply, or add your own.

❑ This is how it was done in our families of origin; we followed suit.
❑ Force of habit. This is the way we started out in early marriage, and it just stuck.
❑ Neither of us wanted to be involved with finances, so the spouse who objected least is the financial manager.
❑ The person with the strongest interest in money matters takes the lead.
❑ Other _____

The lack of training in finances — a fundamental and critical area of marriage — is serious enough, but combined with little or no communication, the situation can be disastrous. If a husband and wife know how to communicate, the natural balance will often keep them out of financial trouble. For example, a wife may have a decided fear of being in debt and normally exercises restraint. If she finds herself in financial trouble, she will try to seek help and do what is necessary to correct the situation. In the same marriage, the majority of serious debts may result from the husband's spending. All too often his indifference, pride, or eternal optimism keeps him from seeking help initially.

What is the situation in your marriage? Do you have a natural balance between husband's/wife's inclinations that keeps your finances in check? If so, describe.

_____

_____

_____

JESUS SAID...

Week 5, Day 4

HUSBAND-WIFE COMMUNICATIONS *continued . . .*

Notes

Few families desire or plan financial problems. Most mishaps occur because of poor training, poor communication, and/or a childhood of conditioned desires. Too often, parents don't teach their children that their lifestyle was earned by many years of effort and usually started with several years of sacrifice. Equipped with a value system learned in a generally affluent home and with a handful of credit cards, many young couples set out to duplicate or to improve on their parents' success. The result in the majority of marriages today is disaster.

If you are married, pray with your spouse. Thank God for your similarities and for your differences. Ask Him to show you how to use those to bring about financial health in your marriage. If single, pray with a friend about how you can learn from this introspection.

It may be that you, or one of your extended family members, have already suffered a divorce where money problems played a key role in the breakup. What lessons can you take from this experience and apply to your current situation?

_____

_____

_____

_____

_____

_____

If you are a parent (or planning to be one!), list at least two ways you can model good communications in the area of money management.

_____

_____

_____

_____

_____

Week 5, Day 4

Notes

JESUS SAID...

TURNING THINGS AROUND

Scripture Verses

"Plans fail for lack of counsel, but with many advisers they succeed."
—*Proverbs 15:22*

The first step in turning around an out-of-balance marriage is to recognize that "different" does not mean "inferior." God put different gifts and abilities in the marriage, and it takes two people working as one to succeed in the home. Since one member of the married duo — often, but not always, the husband — may exclude the other mate from financial decisions, a concerted effort must be made to use that other person's gifts and abilities, particularly as a counselor. Remember, a counselor does not scream, cry, or throw temper tantrums! Emotional expressions dampen honesty, and honesty between partners is an absolute necessity. Almost anyone can deal with a situation if the person knows about it and is part of the planning. When deceptions later show up as crises, distrust occurs.

Step #1: Getting Help — If the financially-related marital problems and the communication gap are intense, most couples will need outside help to get on the right track. Singles can also benefit greatly from wise counsel. Seeking godly counsel for marriage or financial problems can be as natural as seeking medical help. The verse at left suggests that wise counsel invites success.

Write the initials of the person or persons whose help you seek in the following categories:

_____	medical doctor	_____	electrician
_____	attorney	_____	auto mechanic
_____	financial counselor		mental-health
_____	plumber	_____	professional

To decide where to turn for help:

- Ask your pastor/church-staff members to give you the names of available, qualified counselors. For financial needs, these referals may be trained financial counselors or seasoned business people from your church.

- Ask friends whom you know have received counseling to provide you names of professionals whose counsel proved effective.

- Meet with a volunteer Christian financial counselor (such as those trained by LifeWay or Christian Financial Concepts).

Week 5, Day 5

- Call Consumer Credit Counseling Service of Atlanta at 1-888-771-HOPE. A credit counseling service can help you by structuring a debt repayment plan that is realistic and manageable. They do this by directly intervening with your creditors to negotiate lower monthly payments and to reduce, and sometimes eliminate, accruing interest charges.

Seek the mentoring of other couples or individuals who have been through financial crises and who have found God's solutions. Likewise, if you have experiences to share that would help others, let this be known, so others will realize they can turn to you. The function of the body of Christ is to minister to others within the body as needs arise. See what the Bible says in the verse at right about waging such struggles alone.

What couple comes to mind as you think of seeking financial mentors? Jot down the initials of this duo. _____

Step #2: Setting Specific Goals — Couples should plan a weekend alone together so they can discuss every aspect of the family's finances and agree on specific goals. Remember that any financial planning involves two people seeking mutually compatible goals under the umbrella of God's plan for their lives. Two people operating as one with unity of mind will find God's plan. In the same way, single persons can use these steps to find God's plan. See the verse at right.

You may need to reach an agreeable compromise when you establish goals. One member of the duo may be more committed to giving than the other; a sofa may be more important to one, while a bass boat seems like a basic necessity to the other! Here are some suggestions for reaching compromise.

a. Discern God's overall plan; adjust as necessary to make it work.

b. Find the answers both spouses can agree on first, write them down, and pray about them before you move on to more controversial areas.

c. When an impasse is reached over any area, such as food, clothing, or education, each should list five positions from his or her best to worst. Then they discard their first and last and find one of the other three they can agree on.

"Two are better than one, because they have a good return for their work. If one falls down, his friend can help him up. But pity the man who falls and has no one to help him up!"
—Ecclesiastes 4:9-10

"I love those who love me, and those who seek me find me."
—Proverbs 8:17

JESUS SAID...

TURNING THINGS AROUND *continued . . .*

Scripture Verses

**A time in which I or my spouse and I could schedule this getaway is
_____. A place it could be is _____.**

Step #3: Tackling Problems — If you are single, establish goals in light of what you have studied and share them with a trusted friend. In the case of a couple, if problems exist, the husband must assume the burden of direct creditor control — acting as a buffer for his wife. That doesn't mean the wife is not involved but that he is the visible interface. A great cause of fear in a marriage, and ultimately strife, is creditor pressure. Often the husband fears that his wife cannot make adjustments to reduce spending. Usually, the opposite is true. If a husband will provide direction and submit to the same controls, his wife will adjust as necessary. Communication and planning are the keys to success. Determine where you are financially, develop a plan that is fair to both, and talk about it calmly.

"Be completely humble and gentle; be patient, bearing with one another in love."
—*Ephesians 4:2*

Read the Scripture at left. Below, list a specific way each of you can "be patient, bearing with one another in love" in the area of money matters.

(Husband) _____
(Wife)_____

Step #4: Bookkeeping — In a healthy marriage, the task of recordkeeping falls to the spouse best equipped to do it, assuming that no major financial problems exist. Sometimes this is the person with the most time; sometimes it is the one who is the most meticulous. In one home, a husband managed the finances because he was a bookkeeper by trade, and his doing so was logical. In another marriage in which the husband had an accounting-related profession, his wife kept the books to guard her husband from "overkill" — too much money detail at both home and office. Regularly, the record keeper can review the books with the non-record-keeping mate.

On a separate sheet, list the pros and cons of each spouse handling the bookkeeping. What are the qualities/circumstances that make you/your spouse the ideal/least suitable person to keep family financial records?

Week 5, Day 5

Step #5: Children's Discipline — Establishing financial discipline in children is difficult, if not impossible, unless both parents agree on goals and enforce rules consistently. Parents can't wait until a situation arises to see if they agree. They must meet it with a unified front. If the family has a rule that children earn at least one-half of all clothing money, and Mom slips them money without Dad's knowledge, they learn a double lesson: slothfulness pays, and authority can be manipulated. Eventually, an employer will correct that notion for them swiftly.

Describe a time in which spousal disagreement about discipline yielded an unpleasant consequence in your home or in your childhood home.

_____

_____

_____

_____

Remember, neither spouse is always right or wrong. Balance is the key, and God provides it through both husband and wife.

Of the five areas mentioned in today's work, put a star by the one you consider the most difficult for you in your life. Then, humbly approach the throne of grace, asking God to help you turn this area of weakness into your area of strength.

As you pray, go "knee to knee" with your spouse in prayer. Turn your chairs so your knees touch. Clasp both hands. If you are single, join a friend for prayer time. Talk with your partner about ways you feel the Lord might be speaking to you through this lesson. Then spend some time praying about what God has put on your heart.

JESUS SAID...

HOW TO PROSPER FROM PROBLEMS

This Week

Scripture Verses

"Consider it pure joy, my brothers, whenever you face trials of many kinds."

—James 1:2

Either you've had some financial difficulties yourself, or you've seen others in financial turmoil, and you want to avoid their mistakes. Perhaps you have grown children that you're concerned about; you want to learn ways you can help them avoid debt. The majority of Americans have experienced financial discouragement, want to avoid it, or want to help others through it.

I often counsel Christians who are discouraged over their problems. Many are discouraged to the point of divorce — and some to suicide. Satan knows where you're vulnerable. In today's America, that vulnerability usually involves self-esteem and financial security.

Discouragement abounds when others appear to be doing well and you are not. When everyone is poor, people can adjust more readily to that. But when someone has lost a job and most of his or her friends still have theirs, being jobless is very difficult. High debt loads and creditor pressures add to the feelings of inadequacy and failure.

In a land of plenty like ours, even those who are poor are better off than the majority of the world's people. Among poor households in the U.S., a great percentage are buying their homes, own a car, and have color televisions. So why do you feel despair and discouragment? Because you've adjusted your expectations and made them relative to everyone else around you. It's the same symptom that causes despair in a multimillionaire whose assets have shrunk to a few hundred thousand.

As a Christian, you may sometimes fear that your problems will make others think of you as less spiritual. However, we've actually come full circle from those Christians of the first and second centuries who believed that problems evidenced spiritual depth. Although neither extreme is scripturally correct, the case for Christians undergoing problems is more scriptural. See the verse at left. The trials that James addresses are a consequence of serving God uncompromisingly. Most people's current problems result from violating biblical principles, particularly those relating to money.

Week 6, Day 1

As you have gone through the previous weeks in this study, have you been able to identify any biblical principle(s) pertaining to money you have violated that may have resulted in your problem? If so, identify it (or them) below.

_____

_____

_____

_____

Perhaps the most consistent area of discouragement for most people is financial failure. Not only is your ego involved with your ability to provide, but your security is also threatened. Often the demonstration of a Christian's stewardship is not how much he or she gives but how the person reacts when there is not much to give. With many, if not most Christians, their faith at any given time seems proportional to their material resources. Not for all, obviously. Some Christians find that in the midst of their most difficult times, their faith grows and matures, which is exactly what James 1:3 at right says will happen if you abide in Christ.

"Because you know that the testing of your faith develops perseverance."
—*James 1:3*

The greatest threat to your service to God is being sidetracked into a preoccupation about success. God can allow financial crises to come into your life to give you the opportunity to decide whom you really serve. Jesus (see the verse at right) teaches that a Christian cannot divide loyalties. You *will* serve but one God.

"No one can serve two masters. Either he will hate the one and love the other, or he will be devoted to the one and despise the other. You cannot serve both God and Money."
—*Matthew 6:24*

As you have made your way through your most recent financial trial, have you determined that you may have been serving another god besides the One True God? Check any of the phrases below that describe the god you have served.

- ❑ Others' perception of me
- ❑ A desire to achieve, career-wise
- ❑ A desire to overcome an impoverished childhood
- ❑ A love of owning things
- ❑ Other _____

JESUS SAID...

HOW TO PROSPER FROM PROBLEMS *continued . . .*

Scripture Verses

"And anyone who does not carry his cross and follow me cannot be my disciple."
—Luke 14:27

You signed a contract with God when you made Christ Lord over your life and gave God the right to do whatever is necessary to keep you on His path. See what Jesus said about this in the verse at left. So, rather than immediately seeking to escape a financial difficulty, first determine what faults God can correct in you if you turn to Him in your time of need.

Are you already able to sense that God was trying to correct a pattern or a mindset in your life as He worked through your recent financial difficulty? If so, describe what you've observed.

_____

_____

_____

_____

An old cliché summarizes this area: "Keep on keeping on." Decide what you believe, and trust God regardless of outside circumstances. Determine in advance your response to any situation. If anyone, Christian or otherwise, waits until a problem occurs to decide how he or she will deal with it, events will control the person's response, not God's Word.

Can you think of a time in which you determined in advance how you would respond before a financial temptation or difficulty struck? If so, describe what happened.

_____

_____

_____

_____

You might have answered that you committed in advance to stay out of stores as much as possible in order to avoid unwise or impulse purchases. You might have determined you would say no if a friend asked you to go shopping, or you might have agreed to go only with an accountability partner to help you stick to your intended mission, instead of spending frivolously.

Week 6, Day 1

God gives you many biblical examples of people who faced difficult situations. Some collapsed in self-pity, while others grew stronger. Name some who were doers of the Word instead of merely listeners only (as James 1:22 at right specifies).

_____

_____

_____

_____

You may have mentioned some "doers" such as Abraham, Nehemiah, Daniel, and Paul — certainly not perfect people but definitely obedient ones. In difficult times, they did not panic or become depressed; they turned to the Lord. Some of them weren't rescued immediately. Some even died. But remember this: so did everyone else. If all you're looking for is what you can have in this world, then you've missed the blessing. God wants to bless you with peace in this life and eternal rewards in the next.

One of the ways to stay out of debt is to stay focused on the Lord. Even if you get on a budget and take all the previously-mentioned steps, times of discouragement will still occur. Make your directional choice today (see the verse at right), so when tough times roll around again, you won't have to stop and make that commitment.

Thank the Lord for how He has used this difficulty of your financial circumstances to show you a better way. If you haven't experienced a recent financial plight, then think of some other life event in which you've learned and grown. Thank Him.

"Do not merely listen to the word, and so deceive yourselves. Do what it says."
—James 1:22

"Choose for yourselves this day whom you will serve."
—Joshua 24:15b

"Therefore we also, since we are surrounded by so great a cloud of witnesses, let us lay aside every weight, and the sin which so easily ensnares us, and let us run with endurance the race that is set before us . . . ."
—Hebrews 12:1

JESUS SAID...

Week 6, Day 2

KEEPING CHRIST IN CHRISTMAS

Scripture Verses

W hy devote an entire day's study to Christmas, you might ask? Because it's a proven fact that holiday spending can derail an otherwise solid financial strategy, unless you plan carefully. One of the ways to stay out of financial trouble is to plan all year long for Christmas, making Christmas a lifestyle that ensures that Christ remains at the center of the holiday season.

I feel cheated when I see Christ being taken out of Christmas. That occurs with both Christians as well as with non-Christians. Even Christians have adjusted to the holiday season's commercialism. Don't get me wrong. I'm not an opponent of the holiday time. This season provides opportunities for families to reunite and also provides a pleasant break from our routines. I personally look forward to these days as opportunities to visit with friends who are much too busy other times of the year to stop and relax.

But you may find that you have become terribly imbalanced in your approach to Christmas. You give a myriad of useless gifts at Christmas because you feel that doing so is expected of you, and you feel guilty if you don't. The commercialized world now makes a $100 toy seem perfectly normal. You may be depressed if you can't provide the latest indulgences to your children or grandchildren. The closer you get to Christmas Day, the more unworthy you feel if you can't indulge.

Unfortunately the pressure doesn't end once Christmas is past, either. Those who can't afford to compete in their gift-giving often dread congregating with their friends immediately after the holidays, because at "show and tell" time, they don't have much to show. Because society is competitive, people often determine a person's worth by his or her ability to buy things. If you've fallen into that trap, study the verse at left.

Go back and read the previous paragraphs. Underline sentences or phrases that describe the pressure you feel at times during the Christmas season.

"For you died and your life is now hidden with Christ in God."
—Colossians 3:3

Week 6, Day 2

Sometimes people balance one extreme by going to the opposite extreme. However, you can't correct the Christmas distortion by eliminating all gift-giving and by observing Christmas as a totally "religious" holiday. You can swing back toward the middle and eliminate the need to compete. Then you will have the freedom to develop God's plan for your family, without the pressure from the commercial world.

As a Christian, you can feel confident that God's plan is different from that of the world and is more, not less, fulfilling. Sometimes people wrongly think that if they deny themselves the "good life," they are better Christians. That's like saying that all drugs are evil. If you absolutely refuse to use drugs, you may experience much pain if you have to have a broken leg set. The harmful, abusive use of drugs is certainly to be avoided. The key, as always in God's plan, is balance. Balance occurs when you follow God's wisdom.

Have you ever done what the above paragraph described? Did you suddenly stamp out all gift-giving or any secular observance at Christmas? What occurred? How do you feel about it now?

_____

_____

_____

_____

_____

_____

_____

_____

Here are some steps to establish a better balance.

1. **Stamp out Santa Claus.** Christian parents can let their children know that Santa is a myth. Santa's harmless, you say? Not so, when parents knowingly deceive their children about an apparently omnipotent being who travels the world in the wink of an eye and disburses presents on the basis of good and bad. It may be a small matter, but it is a place to start.

JESUS SAID...

Week 6, Day 2

Scripture Verses

KEEPING CHRIST IN CHRISTMAS *continued . . .*

2. **Stamp out disharmony.** Husband and wife can pray together and agree on a reasonable gift-giving amount. Once you have reached a decision that you believe represents God's plan for your family, don't get caught by Satan's condemnation as Christmas approaches. The pressure to buy when everyone else is buying will be difficult to resist unless you both absolutely agree. Develop a balanced attitude that will accomplish your goals in the next few years.

It is a good idea to establish a Christmas account and set aside a designated amount each payday that will accumulate in this account. Watch for sales and catalog shop during the year as you discover gift items at reasonable prices. By Christmas all your purchases will have been made in cash, stress will be elimated, and no debts will hang on past January. You can even gift wrap the items as you purchase them — to avoid that later when time is limited.

Many families commit to spend an amount equal to what they spent on gifts to feeding the truly needy or to giving to missions. An amount equal to most of our gift purchases would install a water well in a third-world country, provide a missionary with needed literature, or feed and clothe a family for several months. See the verses at left.

3. **Stamp out credit.** As harmful as commercialized Christmas is, commercialized Christmas on credit cards is even worse. Many families literally indenture themselves to creditors for a whole year just to buy some useless stuff at Christmas.

As Christians we can decide if we *really* serve the God of the universe. If so, He knows our needs and will meet them through His people, without indebtedness. I know some people reading this have some desperate needs. I also know that others sincerely want to help but don't know who has needs. Using credit allows those who have needs to temporarily buffer themselves from God's real source. I believe Satan has used credit cards to cheat God's people out of blessings and to keep them in bondage.

"Do not withhold good from those who deserve it, when it is in your power to act."
—*Proverbs 3:27*

"And if anyone gives even a cup of cold water to one of these little ones because he is my disciple, I tell you the truth, he will certainly not lose his reward."
—*Matthew 10:42*

Week 6, Day 2

What kind of decision(s) did you make as you read the previous three suggestions? Describe below.

_____

_____

_____

_____

If you agreed with the "Why bother?" question posed at the beginning of today's work, I trust you are now able to understand the Christ-in-Christmas issue as it relates to finances. Gift-giving is one area totally under your control, and it is a leaven that Satan sprinkles in the church. Giving gifts is not the problem, just as the use of credit is not the problem. However, the misuse of these things entangles you and diverts your attention from Christ to material things.

You may be trying to negotiate a compromise with an enemy who is totally dedicated to destroying you. As a Christian, you can decide to draw a battle line again. You can declare: I will keep Christ foremost in Christmas and will balance spending and giving as He directs.

In the area of keeping Christmas spending and holiday observances within balance, what are some suggestions that have worked for you? Write two here. Prepare to share them with the group.

_____

_____

_____

_____

"Command those who are rich in this present world not to be arrogant nor to put their hope in wealth, which is so uncertain, but to put their hope in God, who richly provides us with everything for our enjoyment."
     —1 Timothy 6:17

JESUS SAID...

AVOIDING TEMPTATION

This Week

Scripture Verses

"Be self-controlled and alert. Your enemy the devil prowls around like a roaring lion looking for someone to devour."
            —1 Peter 5:8

"For our struggle is not against flesh and blood, but against the rulers, against the authorities, against the powers of this dark world and against the spiritual forces of evil in the heavenly realms."
            —Ephesians 6:12

" . . . When he lies, he speaks his native language, for he is a liar and the father of lies. "
            —John 8:44b

Just because you complete this course, set up a workable budget, and pledge to turn over a new financial leaf doesn't mean all will be smooth sailing! You won't stop being vulnerable. Satan will still try to lay a trap for you to get you off course as you run the race. You have been tempted in the past, and you will experience temptation again. In today's work, you'll develop a practical plan to overcome temptation.

Why would Satan want to derail you? Actually, a better question is, why wouldn't he? During the past five weeks, you've gone from a "me-centered" outlook to a Christ-centered one. You've been challenged to be trustworthy with your resources. You've become aware that all you thought you possess is actually God's. You've been attracted to the financial freedom that serving God faithfully can provide. Satan is always looking for ways to stop you short of your goals. The first step, then, is to be aware of Satan's schemes.

Read the verses appearing in the margin. Below, describe ways you have experienced Satan's attack in the area of money management — maybe even as you've begun this study.

_____

_____

_____

_____

Perhaps you answered something like this: I experience temptation when I believe that I "must have" a certain possession even though I know, deep within me, that I don't need it. I become greedy and envious when I see others' belongings and want the same things. I fall off track when I fail to keep good records or fail to shop purposefully and economically.

The Bible says it clearly: Satan is waiting to devour you, to prove to you that you can't overcome temptation. You don't fight a flesh-and-blood foe but a foe in the spiritual realm. Satan is the father of lies, and he will try to convince you that your time in this course has been wasted.

Week 6, Day 3

The good news is, you can defeat the prince of darkness. No temptation, in the area of money management or in any other area, for that matter, is too great for you to conquer with God's help. See the verses at right.

What does Matthew 4:1 mean when it says that Jesus was tempted?

_____
_____
_____
_____

Do you believe that God has promised to provide a way out of temptation?

_____

Do you believe that the One in you is stronger than is the tempter?

_____

Below, describe a time in which you experienced God's power to overcome temptation in financial matters.

_____
_____
_____
_____

Perhaps you've had an experience like one woman I know. She was at a checkout counter, about to purchase three knit shirts. She reasoned that the shirts were discounted, that she was buying them at a resale shop, and that the clothes she had just sold at a consignment store would more than cover the purchases. Then she remembered 1 Corinthians 10:13, at right. She realized that she needed to apply the consignment check to another, more urgent budget item, rather than to buy the shirts. She put them back on the rack and thanked God for providing His wisdom.

Scripture Verses

"Then Jesus was led by the Spirit into the desert to be tempted by the devil . . . . Jesus said to him, 'Away from me, Satan! For it is written: "Worship the Lord your God, and serve him only."'"
—Matthew 4:1, 10

"You, dear children, are from God and have overcome them, because the one who is in you is greater than the one who is in the world."
—1 John 4:4

"And God is faithful; he will not let you be tempted beyond what you can bear. But when you are tempted, he will also provide a way out so that you can stand up under it."
—1 Corinthians 10:13b

JESUS SAID...

Notes

AVOIDING TEMPTATION *continued . . .*

Here are some tips for overcoming financial temptation.

1. **Memorize Scripture**, so that God's Word comes to mind in times of temptation, just as it did for the lady buying the shirts. Hide these words in your heart, and the Holy Spirit will use them to help you overcome the enemy.

2. **Be aware of deception.** One sure way to fail is to deceive yourself into believing you're too strong to fail. Avoid an air of superiority. Just because you've learned some godly principles in this course doesn't mean you're not still vulnerable.

3. **Be accountable.** All Christians can be accountable to others, so that when we stray off the path someone else will correct us. A trusted friend may serve as your accountability partner. Often, the best accountability comes within the home, especially between husband and wife. If they have an open and honest relationship, one will detect the other's slip-ups quickly. Correcting must be done gently and in love, or the result will be bitterness. Children (or grandchildren) will participate wholeheartedly in the detection and correction process. (Mine never fail to detect when I exceed the posted speed limit.) Frequently this study has suggested taking someone with you when you shop. A support group, such as the members with whom you are studying this material, is helpful to discuss challenges, even after the study ends. Often groups remain bonded for months and even years, and members remain accountable to each other.

4. **Constantly ask yourself the question, "How much is enough?"** At the cash register, as you put items in your grocery cart, as you respond to telephone sales pitches, as you order from catalogs, ask yourself, "Is this a want or a need? Where would God want me to draw the line?"

5. **Shun evil.** Take a different route if you think you might be tempted to browse the new car lots, the travel agencies with their compelling brochures, the accessory boutiques, or wherever your weakness lies. Get yourself removed from catalog mailing lists. Avoid walking by perfume counters. Avoid grocery shopping when you're hungry. Get unnecessary TV cable channels removed. Be proactive in removing stumbling blocks.

Week 6, Day 3

6. **Quickly confess.** Whenever you detect a deception in your own life, large or small, stop what you're doing and confess it immediately. That means not only to God but to those who observe you or those your decision has impacted. If your overspending in the clothing area has kept your spouse from getting his or her fair share, tell him or her that you're sorry. Make amends promptly. Don't always assume that the others involved will understand or accept an apology. It is not necessary for them alone. It is also for you. See the verse at right.

Below write two other tips that you've already put into practice to eliminate temptation. Be prepared to share one of them with the group.

_____

_____

_____

_____

_____

_____

Ask your accountability partner to pray with you about this area of temptation. Thank God for sending you this person to help you. In the presence of your partner, ask God to be an ever-present help and a clear, distinct voice when you're tempted to stumble.

Based on the verses you've studied this week, what do you believe Jesus is saying to you personally about debt?

_____

_____

_____

_____

"He who conceals his sins does not prosper, but whoever confesses and renounces them finds mercy."
—*Proverbs 28:13*

JESUS SAID...

Week 6, Day 4

FINDING MONEY WHERE MONEY ISN'T

"Whoa!" you say, when you look at today's title. "Now that's a way to stay out of debt. But how? I don't know any hidden sources of money." Well, you have them. Everyone does. You can increase your cash flow by reducing your expenses. Your blessings will multiply when you are faithful with the little you have. The apostle Paul wrote, "Now it is required that those who have been given a trust must prove faithful" (1 Corinthians 4:2). By following these tips, and others that you may already have put into practice, you can practice "alternative buying": ways to really make your dollars stretch to the end of the month. Most of all, you'll sense God's hope growing in your life as you bring these aspects of your life under the powerful control of Jesus.

Tip #1: Buy used goods. Do you sometimes feel deprived when you think about buying something previously owned? Contrary to what you might think, acquiring something second hand can be a very positive experience, and making such a purchase does not require a lot of expertise. It does take planning and research. If you know you will need a major appliance or a car, begin shopping three or four months before you plan to replace the item. Consider buying used automobiles, appliances, televisions, furniture, wedding dresses and other formal wear, recreational vehicles, children's clothing, and even tools. Buying a used car doesn't have to turn into a nightmare. Watch bulletin boards at your office or church for "For Sale" signs, and let your need be known to your Sunday School class. Buy from a reliable person who has taken care of his or her car. Ask a mechanic to check it out before purchase, and ask to see service records. Perhaps an older relative who has used a car mainly for in-town errands is selling his or her vehicle prior to moving to a retirement center or is even "trading up." You might offer to buy that person's car, helping out the owner and giving yourself peace of mind about buying a used vehicle.

What apprehensions do you have when you consider this tip? What might you have to overcome to take this step? Is pride part of the issue?

_____

_____

Week 6, Day 4

Tip #2: Shop around. Get more than one estimate before making a major purchase. Prices often vary widely. Use the Yellow Pages or even the Internet to gather information. Sometimes you can use someone else's lower price as a bargaining chip. Apply this principle to auto repairs, auto and homeowners' insurance, film processing, video rental; in fact, it can be applied to just about every area of buying.

Tip #3: Rent. Owning things isn't always best. Renting makes more sense for items like vacation cottages, timeshare arrangements, or major tools like a tiller or chainsaw. Renting avoids depreciation, obsolescence, and property taxes. For recreational property, watch office or church bulletin boards.

Tip #4: Pay cash. Sometimes you can buy an item for less by offering cash instead of using credit. Plunking down cash is more difficult than plastic. Plan ahead to avoid impulse purchases.

Tip #5: Negotiate. Ask the salesperson if the price-tag price is his or her best price. Amazingly, sometimes people will take less for an item. This is especially true for electronics and appliances. Don't pressure, but remember that sometimes you don't *have* because you don't *ask*.

Tip #6: Pay bills when they are due. Goodwill is highly important with merchants. Protect your reputation, your witness, and your credit rating.

In the blanks below, describe a time when one of these tactics has worked for you. Then, before your group meeting, ask a friend to share an experience with you that pertains to one of these tips.

_____

_____

Tip #7: Stockpile anticipated needs. Buy in quantities. Not only is the per-item price usually less, you are preparing for natural disasters, economic downturns, illness, or for others who might have needs. Quantity values can include canned goods, dried foods, paper goods, pet food, and cleaning items, among others. Shop clearance sales, advertised specials in grocery stores, or membership warehouses.

JESUS SAID...

Notes

FINDING MONEY WHERE MONEY ISN'T *continued . .*

Tip #8: Set up a babysitting co-op. Join forces with other couples you know and develop a babysitting plan, trading time on a child-per-child basis.

Tip #9: Don't always shop price. Value includes price and durability. The cheapest is not the first or only criteria. Sometimes being a valued customer at a store pays off, even if you don't always get deep discount prices. In such good-will situations, salespeople may alert you to special sales, unadvertised specials, or future discounts.

Tip #10: Liquidate small assets. Sell off items around the house that you no longer use. Most people do this by hosting a yard or garage sale. Go through every room in the house, especially closets, and look for items that haven't been used in a year. Plan your sale for the first weekend after the first of the month, because most people receive some type of income on the first of the month.

Tip #11: Review everything. Turn your regular expenses inside out to look for ways to cut costs. Can you drop back to weekends-only on your newspaper subscription? Can you cut back on magazines? Can you arrange for automatic payroll deductions for insurance or utilities to save postage? Can you shut your dishwasher off before the drying cycle to save money and energy? Can you iron your own shirts instead of having them laundered? Can you obtain plant cuttings from a friend instead of purchasing them at a nursery? Can you carpool to work or to church events? No expenditure is beyond scrutiny.

By the same token, don't try to squeeze every penny out of every dollar and make saving money some kind of "second religion." After all, those goods and services you purchase provide someone a job. Do make it your aim to be a good steward in order to provide you and your family not with more money but with more freedom — the freedom to give to the Lord's work, to help other people in need, to be flexible in your budget, and to be spontaneous in your spending without being destructive to your overall financial plan.

Ask God to help you avoid taking the easy way out and to genuinely look for cost-cutting measures.

Week 6, Day 4

Notes

JESUS SAID...

Week 6, Day 5

FACING THE FUTURE, JOYFULLY

Scripture Verses

"But he knows the way that I take; when he has tested me, I will come forth as gold."

–Job 23:10

Think back to where you were at the start of the course. At that point, would you have thought you could ever use the word "joyful" to describe your money matters? By now you should be well along in your budgeting process and feeling freer every week. Read this promise from God, appearing at left.

You've been through a tough six weeks, but I believe you have gained skills that can truly make the money-management part of your life a joyful one.

Looking back on your six weeks in this study, zero in on one skill that you believe you have learned that will help you most in the future. Describe it below.

_____

_____

_____

_____

You might have answered that you have learned to pray about every purchase, to determine if God approves of it. Perhaps the practical skill of tracking income in/income out on a monthly basis has helped you most. You may have benefited from money-saving tips or from learning specific ways to avoid temptation. You may have seen how you need to break the cycle of poor financial decision making before it impacts your children.

The goal of this course has been to help you learn life skills that apply across the board, not just money skills. Below, take the skill that you listed above and describe how you believe it will help you in another area of your life. *(Example: The confidence I feel about knowing how to balance my budget also makes me believe I can learn parenting skills more confidently.)*

_____

_____

_____

_____

Week 6, Day 5

After you learn self-control over spending money, you also may see that other areas of your life are out of control. For example, do you struggle with self-control in the areas of:

- ❏ food intake
- ❏ emotions
- ❏ negative thought patterns
- ❏ time management, or
- ❏ sexual behavior?

As you begin to envision yourself as a self-controlled person in the area of money, you can bring other areas of your life under God's control, as well. God can use you as you come under His control. See Luke 12:42 at right.

Yet, even with this new knowledge and added confidence, you may believe you've only scratched the surface in terms of skills you need. Now that you're into this topic, I hope I've managed to whet your appetite for more tips — to learn more about the mechanism that will help you step out of a harmful cycle permanently. For example, since you've taken these first steps, you may now ask questions like:

- What do I do about family loans? Should I borrow money from parents or loan money to a needy relative?

- How do I know whether God would approve of my upcoming business venture?

- What does the Bible have to say about ethical, financial business practices?

- How much should I save? What about other investments?

- I'm contemplating a career change. How will this decision fit into my overall financial picture?

Proverbs 10:14 addresses the biblical outlook on gaining wisdom. Storing up knowledge that will help you have an abundant life is surely biblical.

Scripture Verses

". . . Who then is the faithful and wise manager, whom the master puts in charge of his servants to give them their food allowance at the proper time?"
—Luke 12:42

"Wise men store up knowledge, but the mouth of a fool invites ruin."
—Proverbs 10:14

JESUS SAID...

FACING THE FUTURE, JOYFULLY *continued . . .*

Notes

Go back and put a star by any of the previous questions I've just listed that you still have. Below write other areas in which you desire to explore.

_____

_____

_____

_____

_____

_____

I hope you are already praying about whether God would have you continue in the next book in this series, *Jesus On Money: Making Mid-Course Corrections.* It will lead you through more critical lifestyle adjustments necessary to keep you debt-free for the rest of your life. This will enable you to continue the journey of your lifelong, obedient relationship with Jesus, as you are challenged to be trustworthy with your resources to fulfill God's purposes.

Through His Word, Jesus has given us everything we need to manage our resources successfully and wisely. What is the most significant thing you have discovered Jesus has to say on money?

_____

_____

_____

_____

_____

_____

Congratulations on your diligent work in this course. May God bless you as you continue to follow Him.

Find someone who would benefit from the same skills you've learned. Encourage that person to participate in a Book 1 study of *Jesus On Money*. Ask God to help you be a good steward of the knowledge you've received.

JESUS ON

MONEY

Charts

Monthly Income and Expenses

GROSS INCOME PER MONTH $_____
     Salary $_____
     Interest $_____
     Dividends $_____
     Other $_____

LESS

   1. Tithe $_____

   2. Tax (Estimated — Include Federal, State, FICA) $_____

     NET SPENDABLE INCOME $_____

   3. Housing $_____
     Mortgage (rent) $_____
     Insurance $_____
     Taxes $_____
     Electricity $_____
     Gas $_____
     Water $_____
     Sanitation $_____
     Telephone $_____
     Maintenance $_____
     Other $_____

   4. Food $_____

   5. Automobile(s) $_____
     Payments $_____
     Gas & Oil $_____
     Insurance $_____
     License/Taxes $_____
     Maint./Repair/Replace $_____

   6. Insurance $_____
     Life $_____
     Medical $_____
     Other $_____

   7. Debts $_____
     Credit Card $_____
     Loans & Notes $_____
     Other $_____

Monthly Income and Expenses

8. Entertainment & Recreation $_____

    Eating Out $_____
    Baby Sitters $_____
    Activities/Trips $_____
    Vacation $_____
    Other $_____

9. Clothing $_____

10. Savings $_____

11. Medical Expenses $_____

    Doctor $_____
    Dentist $_____
    Drugs $_____
    Other $_____

12. Miscellaneous $_____

    Toiletry, cosmetics $_____
    Beauty, barber $_____
    Laundry, cleaning $_____
    Allowances, lunches $_____
    Subscriptions $_____
    Gifts (incl. Christmas) $_____
    Cash $_____
    Other $_____

13. School/Child Care $_____

    Tuition $_____
    Materials $_____
    Transportation $_____
    Day Care $_____

14. Investments $_____

TOTAL EXPENSES $_____

INCOME VS. EXPENSES

    Net Spendable Income $_____
    Less Expenses $_____

15. Unallocated Surplus Income $_____

List of Debts

LIST OF DEBTS as of: _____

- **To Whom Owed:** _____
  Contact Name/Phone Number: _____
  Pay Off: _____
  Payments Left: _____
  Monthly Payment: _____
  Due Date: _____

- **To Whom Owed:** _____
  Contact Name/Phone Number: _____
  Pay Off: _____
  Payments Left: _____
  Monthly Payment: _____
  Due Date: _____

- **To Whom Owed:** _____
  Contact Name/Phone Number: _____
  Pay Off: _____
  Payments Left: _____
  Monthly Payment: _____
  Due Date: _____

- **To Whom Owed:** _____
  Contact Name/Phone Number: _____
  Pay Off: _____
  Payments Left: _____
  Monthly Payment: _____
  Due Date: _____

(Make additional copies of page, if needed, to include all debts.)

Budget Analysis

MONTHLY PAYMENT CATEGORY	CURRENT MONTHLY EXPENDITURES	MONTHLY GUIDELINE BUDGET	DIFFERENCE + OR -	NEW MONTHLY BUDGET
1. Tithe				
2. Taxes				
NET SPENDABLE INCOME (Per Month)				
3. Housing				
4. Food				
5. Automobile(s)				
6. Insurance				
7. Debts				
8. Entertainment/Recreation				
9. Clothing				
10. Savings				
11. Medical				
12. Miscellaneous				
13. School/Child Care				
14. Investments				
TOTALS (ITEMS 3-14)				
15. Unallocated Surplus Income				

Percentage Guide for Family Income
(Family of Four)

(The Net Spendable percentages are applicable to Head of Household family of three, as well.)

Gross Household Income	$25,000 or less	$35,000	$45,000	$55,000	$65,000	$85,000	$115,000
1. Tithe	10%	10%	10%	10%	10%	10%	10%
2. Taxes[1]	5.1%	14.9%	17.9%	19.9%	21.8%	25.8%	28.1%
NET SPENDABLE PERCENTAGES BELOW ADD TO 100%.							
NET SPENDABLE INCOME	$21,225	$26,285	$32,445	$38,555	$44,330	$54,570	$71,185
3. Housing	38%	36%	32%	30%	30%	30%	29%
4. Food	14%	12%	13%	12%	11%	11%	11%
5. Auto	14%	12%	13%	14%	14%	13%	13%
6. Insurance	5%	5%	5%	5%	5%	5%	5%
7. Debts	5%	5%	5%	5%	5%	5%	5%
8. Entertainment/Recreation	4%	6%	6%	7%	7%	7%	8%
9. Clothing	5%	5%	5%	6%	6%	7%	7%
10. Savings	5%	5%	5%	5%	5%	5%	5%
11. Medical/Dental	5%	4%	4%	4%	4%	4%	4%
12. Miscellaneous	5%	5%	5%	5%	5%	5%	5%
If you have this expense below, the percentage shown must be deducted from other budget categories.							
13. Investments[2]	—	5%	7%	7%	8%	8%	8%
14. School/Child Care[3]	8%	6%	5%	5%	5%	5%	5%
15. Unallocated Surplus Income[4] —	—	—	—	—	—	—	—

[1] Guideline percentages for tax category include taxes for Social Security, federal, and a small estimated amount for state, based on 2000 rates.

[2] This category is used for long-term investment planning such as college education or retirement. Remember that if you invest, the percentage shown must be deducted from other budget categories.

[3] This category is added as a guide only. If you have this expense, the percentage shown must be deducted from other budgeted categories.

[4] This category is used when surplus income is received. This would be kept in the checking account to be used within a few weeks; otherwise, it should be transferred to an allocated category.

Home Ledger

Date	Ck. #	Transaction	✔	Deposit	Withdrawal	Balance

Individual Account Page

_____ $_____ $_____
ACCOUNT CATEGORY   ALLOCATION   ALLOCATION

Date	Transaction	Deposit		Withdrawal		Balance

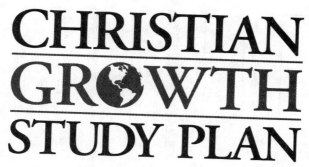

CHRISTIAN GROWTH STUDY PLAN

Preparing Christians to Serve

In the **Christian Growth Study Plan (formerly Church Study Course)**, this book *JESUS ON MONEY – CHARTING A NEW COURSE* is a resource for course credit in the subject area **STEWARDSHIP** of the Christian Growth category of diploma plans. To receive credit, read the book, complete the learning activities, show your work to your pastor, a staff member or church leader, then complete the information on the next page. The form may be duplicated. Send the completed page to:

Christian Growth Study Plan
127 Ninth Avenue, North, MSN 117
Nashville, TN 37234-0117
FAX: (615)251-5067

For information about the Christian Growth Study Plan, refer to the current Christian Growth Study Plan Catalog. Your church office may have a copy. If not, request a free copy from the Christian Growth Study Plan office (615/251-2525).

JESUS ON MONEY – CHARTING A NEW COURSE
COURSE NUMBER: CG- 0558

PARTICIPANT INFORMATION

Social Security Number (USA ONLY)	Personal CGSP Number*	Date of Birth (MONTH, DAY, YEAR)

Name (First, Middle, Last)

Address (Street, Route, or P.O. Box)

| | City, State, or Province | Home Phone | Zip/Postal Code |

CHURCH INFORMATION

Church Name

Address (Street, Route, or P.O. Box)

City, State, or Province   Zip/Postal Code

CHANGE REQUEST ONLY

☐ Former Name

☐ Former Address

City, State, or Province   Zip/Postal Code

☐ Former Church

City, State, or Province   Zip/Postal Code

Signature of Pastor, Conference Leader, or Other Church Leader   Date

*New participants are requested but not required to give SS# and date of birth. Existing participants, please give CGSP# when using SS# for the first time.
Thereafter, only one ID# is required. **Mail to:** Christian Growth Study Plan, 127 Ninth Ave., North, Nashville, TN 37234-0117. Fax: (615)251-5067

Rev. 6-99